BEDSIDE MANNERS

MYTH OF THE DOCTOR-PATIENT RELATIONSHIP

By

CHERYL LEWIS, R.N.

ISBN: 1-4033-7199-7 (e-book)
ISBN: 1-4033-7200-4 (Paperback)

Library of Congress Control Number: 2002094259

This book is printed on acid free paper.

Printed in the United States of America
Bloomington, IN

1stBooks — rev. 11/18/02

TABLE OF CONTENTS

INTRODUCTION

This book is about the travails of what should have been the best of healthcare. Disastrous medical mistakes and the miscalculated attempts to mitigate their damage forced me into an education I would not have undertaken voluntarily. It is not the twelve surgeries and multiple life threatening infections which followed them that are the focus of this book however. The most lamentable story is not my personal trauma but the fact that I am no different from hundreds of thousands of others.

It is up to consumers to safeguard themselves. The healthcare system has proven by its own track record to be incapable of protecting the people whose lives depend upon it. This disregard by the system for consumers is due in part to a surfeit of respect for itself. But equally devastating is the refusal of the system to be accountable to the public for its failures. If there is genius to be found in our medical care today it is in its ability to convince us that it is something better than it is.

Medical care can be no better than the people practicing it. It is therefore important to understand who is providing care, and why they do it the way they do. Becoming knowledgeable about medical care is something everyone can do. Our system of care has its own culture and unveils itself in predictable ways. That which informs our system is discernible in the behaviors and motivations of the individuals working in it today. One can look at the system as a whole to understand how it is made manifest in individuals or look at individual caregivers to understand the system. In practical terms this means that patients who pay attention to the attitudes, motivations and behaviors of workers can learn a great deal about healthcare. Just as importantly consumers can do a great deal to improve their care without technological expertise. It is, in the end, the human interaction between patient and provider that determines how treatment is given and received.

Mahatma Gandhi tells us how to undertake such a study in his autobiography, "It is quite proper to resist and attack a system, but to resist and attack its author is tantamount to resisting and attacking oneself. For we are all tarred with the same brush and are the children of one and the same Creator, and as such the divine powers within us are infinite. To slight a single human being is to slight those divine powers, and thus not only to harm that being but with him the whole world." While there are true incidents described in this book the names and dates are not important. The accounts given are not spectacular. They have been chosen to illustrate that the common everyday problems of healthcare have serious implications for consumers. The little mistakes by physicians are part of the routine and are routinely dismissed. But for patients these issues are not medical minutia.

This is a book about building a better system, not about harming the people in it today. It is truly a book of the tares and the wheat. Clinicians doing a good job for patients are working alongside those who are harming their patients. But it is now time to separate the best from the worst if the harvest of better healthcare is to be realized in the new millennium.

Today the term "healthcare" is more likely to strike terror in the hearts of consumers than it is to provide comfort. Our healthcare system care is about fear. Fear of not having it, losing it if you have it and fear of not being able to afford it. As it undergoes rapid change people working in it fear the loss of what their jobs used to mean as well as the possible loss of their livelihood in the future. It is also about dread. People are afraid of being hurt by a system they don't understand. As a result consumers now are looking for ways to protect themselves from the system.

Patients who dare to criticize the quality of their care fear retaliation from healthcare workers. It is a realistic concern because repercussions directed against patients do occur. This apprehension combined with a painful illness will usually suffice to keep patients silent in the presence of their caregivers. But they do express themselves to others outside the system. I have experienced the very worst that our system has to offer. But having been through it and survived I know that the correct place to put one's faith is in the truth. It is there that the tools for coping with future experience are to be found.

Therefore, let me say that which others dare not say. Allow me to provide a forum for discussing those issues which are vital to obtaining good healthcare. Simply put, I wrote this book because it was the right thing to do. It is meant to give a voice to those who are not able speak for themselves and for those whose voices are now forever silenced.

When the heart speaks however simple the words, its language is always acceptable to all those who have hearts.

Mary Baker Eddy Miscellaneous Writings 1883 - 1896

Chapter 1

Myth of the Doctor Patient Relationship

"Half of what we have taught you is wrong unfortunately, we don't know which half." This is a quote included in a report by Derek Bok President of Harvard medical school in 1983. Today the basis for doctor patient relationships is confusion. Physicians are themselves confounded about what their real role is. For patients the reality of the doctor patient relationship is wildly different than of their physician's. Failure of physicians to promote a positive relationship is a result of how they were taught to think about patients. Much of what they have learned about communicating with their patients is outdated and suffused with superiority about themselves. If physicians are unable to discern what is right or wrong about what they have been taught must patients do it for them?

The doctor patient relationship exists only as a myth. Certainly the damaging effects of it on patients are mythic in size and scope. The urgent question to be answered is: should consumers continue their quest for a productive relationship with their physician? Or should the relationship be abandoned? Finding the answer is possible only after an in-depth examination of the interrelationship between patient and physician. But the situation cannot be reformed without a strong commitment to understand how medical care is delivered to consumers. The story of American healthcare is a saga about power. Physicians have it, patients don't. However, power does not exist in isolation, it requires the submission of its subjects. There are very few situations in life where the powerful are so strong and the weak so defenseless as in the practice of medicine.

People who are experiencing serious illness must focus their attention and energy on healing. They should not be challenged by the very people who are providing them with care during the recovery process. Nor should they be subjected to the stress caused by the unprofessional attitudes and behaviors of clinicians. But this is what is happening. Consumers may expect physicians to conform to higher ethical standards than others. But just as in other professions physicians may fail to meet high standards. By looking at the attitudes prevalent in individual practitioners we can begin to fully appreciate what is happening at the patient level. Healthcare today is increasingly profit driven and remade in the corporate image. As hospitals trim staff and cut back on procedures patient care is transformed into a product of the mega-corporation. Cost cutting in medical treatment involves life and death decisions, which should be more important than the desire for increased profits. But millions of dollars are spent on advertising to sell healthcare instead of providing it to those who need it most. We have lost sight of the standards that were once the basis of compassion and respect for the individual.

To begin to understand what works and doesn't work in the system, we should know more about the people working in it. For the purposes of our discussion the words patient, client and consumer are used interchangeably. Patient is the universally accepted word, standard in the health professions today. Patient has connotations of subservience and naiveté, which are consistent with the way many healthcare providers approach consumers. It is now more accurate to view physicians as consultants and technicians who specialize in the field of medicine. Modern medicine is traditional business selling the fruits of scientific endeavor and its client-patients are you and me. Unfortunately, our healthcare delivery system does not acknowledge the value of its clients who are supporting the system by creating jobs and contributing to the economy.

A popular concept in the healthcare field today is patient responsibility. This means patients accepting responsibility for their own healthcare decisions and active participation in their care. It has also come to mean accepting the emotional as well as physical consequences of those decisions.

But is this realistic? Consumers, "patients" are not the focal point of our healthcare system. The system does not revolve around us as consumers but rather catches us as on its periphery. Our view of health is validated not by ourselves but the system. As patients, consumers are allowed to take responsibility only for those decisions providers deem us capable of making. Due largely to aggressive public relations patients have been led to believe they are equal partners in the system. However, the public is not permitted to have any substantive influence or input into the system. This creates a nonproductive way of interacting between those who are giving care and those who are receiving care. The system itself is telling us we need a new model for healthcare. The culture field of healthcare is defined first by corporations and to a second lesser degree by the physicians who practice medicine today. The formulation and design of healthcare delivery are matched not with consumer need but driven by economics.

It is unlikely that more analysis of the doctor-patient relationship which excludes consumer input will yield new insights. If anything, this relationship has been over analyzed by psychologists. Providers continue to ignore the criticisms brought by both individual consumers and citizen watch groups. Physicians don't believe patients understand enough about healthcare to judge it. Yet, who is more qualified to interpret quality and quantity of care than those who receive it? More fit to judge both the physical and psychological impact? Patients certainly understand how they feel during and after treatment. The only real expert on the role of the patient is the patient himself. The intersection of individual patient need and the delivery of healthcare takes place after systems are designed and implemented. The function of patient is not as partner but consumer, subject to the availability of goods and services.

It is not enough to design a medical protocol for consumers with scientific fact and fantastic technology. The underlying emotional impact of medical procedures is also an integral part of the treatment. The effects that the behavior of healthcare workers produce in their patients have long been ignored. But patients realize that the physical benefit of treatment can be offset by the emotional damage done to them by clinicians. Healthcare workers respond to patients as they have taught to. But this way of relating to patients is ineffectual because patients are individuals. Each interaction between physician and patient must express that individuality. When it doesn't patients feel misunderstood and unimportant.

But after the emotional and intellectual frustration how do consumers regroup and redirect the course of their recovery? One significant consumer response is reflected by popular interest in the current mind-body-spirit phenomena. This search is the natural outgrowth of the need for more and better healing. But just as importantly consumers want a form of healthcare that makes room for positive, individual interaction. The search for alternative methods is as much a desire for consideration and personal respect as it is for physical healing.

Spiritual healing too is emerging with renewed interest in mainstream churches. The issue of spirituality and its place in healthcare is becoming more complex primarily due to the intractable position of research to see the world as only science defines it.

Responding to this patient interest a few physicians are beginning to re-examine their own views about the mental aspects of illness. But also physicians would like to explain the sudden, unexpected recovery of some patients who have relied on spiritual resources. Spiritual healing continues to be discounted by physicians not so much because science cannot offer an explanation for it, but because its healings are an embarrassment to science. Spirituality remains a popular issue because its efficacy has universal appeal. When it is used by the patient its free, if it is provided by a practitioner it may be covered by insurance and also be tax deductible.

As a few physicians begin to integrate the role of mind and religion into their view of patients so too do patients look at their physicians in a new way. In an excellent book by Richard Nennemen, former editor of the Christian Science Monitor, The New Birth of Christianity, he writes:

> "The natural tendency of the human mind, until it has become accustomed to thinking in spiritual terms of reference, is to make some accommodation for the old beliefs of materiality along with the light that is coming in from a new source."

One result of this is that the current doctor-patient relationship has become outmoded. The old, usually inadequate way that physicians have interacted with patients has left this relationship in disturbing disarray. Whether it will survive the rigors of such a rapidly changing (some say deteriorating) system is yet to be determined. The twenty-first century will be a time to study the role that mind plays in illness and recovery from the consumer perspective. Mind has a direct effect on healing, and we know that the negative and positive attitudes of the people around us can also influence recovery.

One overlooked aspect of our system is that it is extremely critical of its patients. The personal appearance and social status of patients are subject to the bigoted and unfair judgmental actions of clinicians. These may be subtle incidents that go unnoticed by patients such as when workers put negative remarks into the patient chart. Or they may be more overt and extreme such as refusing care altogether in the case of low income patients. People who are educated and making a good salary but are unable to get health insurance are also seeing this new form of discrimination. People are experiencing rude behavior and deliberately delayed treatment if they are treated. Both patients on Medicaid and people without insurance are now second class citizens.

Our healthcare is a putative system. It assumes that the people working in it function to promote our best interests. That only the system itself can evolve what is best for us is the psychological basis for American healthcare. It is taken for granted that we have no choice but to trust those who are providing us with care. The blind trust that results between system and user creates an unhealthy dependency on the system by consumers. People are being forced to make health decisions based not on understanding but simple trust in what physicians tell them. To complicate matters insurance companies and health maintenance organizations have severely restricted the availability of care. The combined result is that consumer decisions are made by dictated choice.

But if one wants to make an informed choice about doctors, hospitals or treatment options how does a person know who or what to trust in such a complex system? How can someone without specific technical expertise determine if they are in safe, skilled hands? The answer is in a more astute and confident consumerism. Patients have their own immune system physiology, the will to heal and emotional stamina with which to fight illness. This constitutes a powerful potential for healing in patients. But when physicians demean patients with poor behavior and superior attitudes they decrease the will to heal and create unnecessary emotional stress for patients. Patients must decide if the net effect of those providing medical care increase or decrease their personal healing potential. By changing our current perspective of physicians and the people who work for them we can shed light on a misunderstood system. Learning how particular individuals function in the healthcare setting can begin to make it one where the center point of the system is the consumer not the provider.

Healthcare is not just technology and clinical protocol. It is also a pathological methodology, sometimes benign sometimes malignant. Attitudes, judgments, and personalities overlay a core of clinical expertise and technology that promises quick diagnosis and cure. Just as importantly it is a system that can be used to impose its own brand of ethics and mores on consumers. Physicians can and do increase the pain and suffering of their patients in this way. The patient with a chemical dependency, whether in recovery or not is a prime target for this. Consider the forty-two year old patient with cardiomyopathy (heart disorder) who was terminally ill. This can be an extremely painful way to die. But because this man was an addict his physician refused to provide him with the drugs that could have relieved most of his pain and let him have a comfortable transition from life to death. This physician took it upon himself to be judge and jury and imposed a particularly inhumane sentence. His dictum was that physicians should not provide narcotic drugs to patients who are addicts. But his thinking was as rudimentary as it was merciless. Underlying his decision was his view that people with dependency problems are not the caliber of patients he wanted to treat. The nurses who were involved in his care fought to get their patient some modicum of comfort and compassion from his physician. The patient, his family and his nurses were not served by this man dying in agony. Society was not better off for his suffering, rather it was diminished by the actions of one doctor who saw his idea of the doctor patient relationship as the only right one.

Arnold Mindell Ph.D. the eminent psychologist writes in his book Coma: The Dreambody Near Death,

I called the hospital and explained to the doctor that I understood it was important to inform a patient that his disease was no longer responding to treatment and that he might die soon. But, I added, the staff should realize that the way they inform the patient has the effect of a hypnotic induction and could be murderous. There are many ways to tell a patient that the treatment is not successful but to tell a patient "you will die soon" is a form of murder.

Doctor Mindell has not exaggerated the influence of language choice and attitude in the treatment of patients. There are many other people working alongside doctors who pick up their attitudes. Thus, the shared attitudes of all types healthcare workers are conveyed to patients. If a physician harbors a dislike for a particular patient, others in his employ are likely to feel the same way. The converse is true as well. If a physician works harder for one patient other clinicians will too. These shared attitudes go beyond the categories of positive and negative, to include every shade and nuance of personality and character.

There are identifiable and predictable patterns of behavior in healthcare workers. Anyone who has had prolonged contact with medical personnel because of a chronic illness or serious injury has felt the effects of these attitudes. Families and friends are certainly as aware as patients are about how the medical milieu can help or hinder healing. In spite of this, healthcare workers believe that how they behave is not under scrutiny by the people they provide care to. But nothing could be farther from the truth because patients are keen observers of human nature. Doctors, nurses, and others don't consider themselves responsible to patients. For them, it is an impersonal medical protocol that they must answer to. The common behavioral barriers to effective communication and good care by clinicians are:

- The priority of task completion, their jobs are about getting the work done.

- The job of caring about patients happens (if at all) after the work is finished.

- A strong denial and lack of appreciation for their patient's awareness and level of comprehension regarding their disease and treatment.

- Relating to patients from a reactive rather than active perspective, which results in an exaggerated knee-jerk defensive response to patients.

- A general unwillingness to consider new ways of relating to patients unless they themselves initiate the change to enhance their own position.

Clinicians who function this way do not perform in an isolated atmosphere. They work side by side with those people who have more evolved personalities and understanding of interpersonal relations. There are always people in healthcare giving good care from whom those who are lacking can learn. So why do so many physicians and the people who work for them persist in destructive patterns? Because they are supported by their co-workers and the system itself even when they are wrong. This is a system accustomed to autonomy. It has no experience at self examination, especially when subjected to outside criticism. The elimination of bad behavior and those who indulge in it requires exposure. This entails the risk of displeasure or retaliation from fellow employees. To stand up for a patient's right to be treated with honesty and dignity demands selfless fortitude from workers. For patient or practitioner to remain silent in the face of disrespect is to miscarry the positive potential of the system. The stewardship of the healthcare system fails in its responsibilities when left to its practitioners alone. Supporting patient rights is difficult and often fruitless as in the case of the ninety year old women left neglected in an urgent care center for four and a half hours. This woman had been brought in by her family at 8:30 am with excruciating abdominal pain, something that always requires serious attention. The intake nurse phoned the doctor's office and spoke to the office nurse informing her doctor about the status of his patient and requesting that he come down to see her. An hour went by with no response from the doctor. The nurse called upstairs to the doctors office once again to reiterate the poor condition of the patient. At this point the office nurse refused to bother the doctor again, saying he knew his patient was downstairs. The patient's condition began to deteriorate, vital signs were not stable and her pain was increasing. Forty minutes later the urgent care nurse went up to the doctors office personally to express her increasing concern for her patient. The family also went upstairs and spoke with the doctor's nurse in their efforts to obtain care for their mother. Throughout it all the office nurse would not relay these concerns of family and staff to the physician. Eventually the doctor did come down at one-thirty, after the office lunch hour. By this time the woman was drifting in and out of consciousness and had to be treated for shock. She was immediately transferred to an acute care facility where she died three days later.

The urgent care nurse was pitted against the office nurse. The office nurse had the power to convey important information to her doctor about a patient but chose instead to protect him from interruption. She rebuffed the family and the nurse that came to her on behalf of the patient. This is a nurse in a position of limited authority who exercises her influence without regard for the welfare of patients. It is understandable however, in view of the fact that she works for a physician who left his patient to suffer in spite of the fact that he had several options. He could have had the urgent care physician examine his patient, he could have ordered lab work and x-rays and had the results called to him, and he could have ordered pain medication after the initial exam. Or he could have made the one-minute walk and examined his patient himself in between office patients. He just simply did not bother to do it. This incident is not about medical care, there was virtually no care given. It is about uncaring people misusing their power.

To providers this is an unimportant story lacking in drama. Just an elderly woman for whom aggressive therapy may not have been the appropriate treatment anyway. In other words little if any harm was done. But she was an important person to herself, her family and the one nurse who tried to do the right thing for her. These types of incidents are readily dismissed by professionals. The elderly are at great risk for this type of dismissive treatment. But these situations are the substance of healthcare. Although these patients may be a low priority in offices and hospitals this is what real treatment is about. Should the quality of care be dependent on the patients' age? If so, consumers have little to hope for as they age.

Each and every interaction between doctor and patient leaves an imprint on patients. This provider imprinting may be beneficial or harmful. Patients understand this to be a part of the disease process but clinicians do not. Nor are they aware of their own behavior as they provide care to patients in any qualitative way. As we move through a complex healthcare system in this book we will learn to identify some of these specific behaviors and the motivations behind them.

Consumers must begin to draw attention to the way healthcare employees conduct themselves. It should never be the patient's responsibility to monitor the behavior of caregivers, but healthcare providers are not doing it. And, not all providers will pay attention to the complaints they get from patients who have been treated badly. Many healthcare settings are hectic and crowded contributing to an already impersonal way of relating. It is in this type of atmosphere where patients are most likely to be mistreated and misunderstood. Patients must consider the behavior factor when they make judgments about how well their treatment is working for them. Citizen watch groups must also become more aware that this, too, is an important part of today's healthcare system.

Healthcare and disease are two parts of one problem. One is not a cure for the other. Lack of healthcare is failed healthcare, and disease is the boundary of modern healthcare. The disease state and the state of our healthcare are mirror reflections of one another. Advancing technology has blurred the division between the two by causing disease and injury in the attempt to provide healing.

Healthcare providers regard patients as outsiders, ignorant of the machinations of healthcare. This initiates a process of ego destruction in patients. The cumulative, negative impact of the system and continuous stress induced by caregivers affects healing potential by reducing the patient's sense of self. Effective healing requires the full involvement of the whole person. To diminish any part of an individual whether mental or physical retards recovery.

True recovery does not leave a patient with a loss of self-esteem. And it is only the patient who knows how he feels after treatment. Take for example the patient with an undiagnosed illness who has been labeled a hypochondriac by his doctors. When physicians fail to make a clear cut diagnosis they often fall back on the behavior of the patient to explain away his stated symptoms. This patient complained of long term fatigue, vague muscle and joint pain, and low grade fevers. Even though these symptoms had persisted over many months it did not aid the diagnosis. The basic tests were done and found to be negative, some were improperly interpreted. However, the physician was satisfied that nothing was seriously wrong with his patient. The patient's frustration with his situation then caused depression unrelated to his physical disease. When the symptoms persisted and repeat exams proved negative the chart began to show him as neurotic and complaining. His physician was not astute enough to order more appropriate diagnostic tests. Some serious diseases will have negative lab findings and doctors know this. A difficult diagnosis should be considered a symptom of disease in itself. This pattern of delayed diagnosis may persist for many years. When the diagnosis is made (in this case fibromyalgia) the patient is still subjected to demeaning treatment because he was previously diagnosed as a hypochondriac. When new physicians read his records what stands out will be his label of hypochondria. The actual diagnosis may even become secondary. Patients internalize these criticisms and may start to doubt their own perceptions. The patient now has to cope with a new disease as well as rebuild his battered self esteem. The validation of patient complaints with an actual diagnosis is not enough to undo the damage done to the psyche of patients. Lupus, Grave's disease and even cancer are only a few of the conditions that can be the basis for this type of treatment. The tragedy is that this happens to thousands of consumers daily.

This systematic, psychological reductionism of patients is not realized by physicians even though it is intrinsic to their practice. It has existed for so long that the system cannot distinguish it as something apart from itself. The psychological damage done to people who rely on the healthcare establishment for long periods is something that must be viewed as intransigent. So pervasive is the ego destruction of patients that it is considered an indigenous quality of medical culture.

Healthcare institutions have accelerated the conversion of the system to one that is wholly dependent on commerce for guidance. A strong profit incentive contributes in a tangible way to the formation of those attitudes that are destructive to patients. Attitudes formed at the top of these corporate structures filter down to influence care at the patient level. One of these is constant pressure on consumers to conform their own needs to the needs of healthcare providers. It is now a system in which providers are supported by patients, rather than a system serving and caring for its patients.

Because the source of this stress is system driven I call this phenomena provider produced stress. While healthcare practitioners will resist this concept, patients recognize it and understand the need to bring this issue to the forefront of any meaningful discussion about healthcare.

Every meeting of doctor and patient is affected by many factors unrelated to direct patient care. The business, records, scheduling, referral, prescriptions and insurance sectors must do their jobs correctly. When they don't the patient must see to it that the problem is corrected before they get the care they need. The physician must also do his job efficiently, safely and competently. If not, it is up to the patient to see it corrected or suffer the consequences. When there is error in any one area the entire system becomes a tangle. There are many parts of the system which are interrelated but independently functioning. For consumers the system is both confused and confusing. Trying to stay aware of everything that will have an impact on their treatment is difficult and very frustrating for patients. The only people in the system who are in a position to experience the system as a continuum are patients. They are the only ones to bear the full burden of the stress it produces.

Our society is composed of many untrained, incompetent workers in all facets of industry. People are so accustomed to mistakes that they expect them to happen. For people who have a long term health problem the magnitude of ineptitude in the system is a chronic source of stress. The problem of incompetence and health is worsened because it is generated by the very people who are supposed to alleviate the physical problems induced by it.

Consumers have been indoctrinated to believe they must control the amount of stress that comes into their lives from the circumstances of their illness. When patients become overwhelmed by the stress of their illness physicians tell them to seek counseling. The task of eliminating system stress is then shifted away from clinicians to patients. There are a great many therapists who will devote their time to working with the chronically ill. But just like physicians they do not realize they also are a cause of the stress which patients experience. Providers are quick to induce stress and even quicker still to avoid taking the responsibility for it. Patients do occasionally complain to their physicians about the frustrations of an incompetent system. But the standard refrain from doctors is "I don't have anything to do with the system, I just treat patients." This is denial at its most obvious. They absolutely do have something to do with stresses induced by the functioning of the entire system. The business of health exists in part to support physicians and their families. More importantly, it is the physician who activates the system on behalf of his patient. Without his orders treatment cannot proceed. They must also realize they are seeing and treating the illnesses induced by the stresses of the system. The projection of provider produced stress from physicians onto to patients is not acknowledged in spite of its prevalence.

It is impossible to overstate the negative emotional and physical impact that the HMO mentality has had. To say that a procedure performed on a patient with the approval of an HMO versus that of one done outside an HMO are the same is an over simplification from the patient's perspective. What must happen during the procedure may be the same medically but the attitudes toward it are not. Negativity engendered by the HMO toward the patient about a procedure can affect its potential outcome. If the patient has had to struggle to win approval for a necessary procedure, his capacity to withstand the rigors of treatment may be diminished. When treatment is delayed due to the approval process the patient's physical condition may worsen and the risk of complications increases. Worry and uncertainty about whether treatment will be allowed always leaves a negative impression on patients. It also has an impact on those practitioners trying to do the right thing for their patients by draining their energy as well. That animosity generated by HMOs and insurance companies have a negative mental impact on everyone involved is only common sense. Struggling with disease is difficult, but the added stress forced on a person who is trying to get treatment can change the endurable into the insurmountable.

What happens to the psyche of doctors and nurses working for HMOs is still an unknown. To maintain their employment people who have their paychecks signed by corporate providers must enforce the standards of those companies. Doctors and nurses are now in a position of having to give up those principles which they were taught to uphold. Clinicians have capitulated to the profit motive.

One example of this is the loss of confidentiality. This is a basic moral right for all patients no matter who pays the bill. This is especially troubling when patients want a second opinion. The first doctor must authorize the visit to another doctor. The most important reason for a second evaluation is to gain a fresh, unprejudiced look at a problem, not an opinion construed by the first one. When your doctor okays a visit for a second opinion and chooses that physician the likelihood is that it will be an echo of the first. This loss of basic privacy is stressful and demeaning. Nor is it something patients should be forced to accept.

Healthcare is not something that should just be maintained. It is more than that, good health is dynamic and adaptive. Should healthcare be less? Forcing workers to support these decisions will affect everyone in healthcare professions. It is only a matter of time before we are left with a value system that does not support adequate patient care.

Chapter 2

MD, Medical Doctor or Medical Deity?

Physicians fail to identify with their patients. Instead their self-perspective derives not from a common humanity but what it means to be a medical professional. Their point of reference is the system they work in, not those people seeking their advice. This position is important to understand because it influences where physicians put their energies and allegiance. Identification with their job forms their arena of action. This means that what they do to and for patients is shaped by the context of the physician's workplace. The patient has become something to be molded and fit into the healthcare system. When physicians put patients first they manage the system to benefit their patients. These physicians answer to patients and their needs first, not the system's. Trying to be pro-patient and pro-system at the same time is rarely possible. But unless and until physicians become active in changing the system patients will remain caught in a tug of war between system and patient need.

In our system patients serve as the caryatids, satisfying physicians intellectually and economically. Thus, the doctor patient relationship is not a relationship at all. Rather, it is a complicated business arrangement. Its character and form stems from a complex set of standards set by physicians, lawyers, government regulations and corporations. The ethics and mores of healthcare are now a construct of cold logic untouched by the awareness of human suffering. Care has become so restrictive that the outcome of an office visit can almost be predicted before the visit takes place. The treatment patients get is virtually dictated by insurance companies. Every set of symptoms has its own protocol or way to be treated. The way a patient condition is analyzed is designed by HMOs and insurance carriers.

Most of the time the insurance companies and standards of good medical practice coincide. Medical practices have become insurance practices. As insurance companies become more entwined with medical corporations the separation between medicine and insurance is lost.

The first step toward improvement in such a rigid framework is the realization by patients that equality between patient and physician is right and reasonable. It is also a radical point of view. Without it, patients are forced to exclude from their care those positive characteristics of themselves that contain their real healing potential. Physicians are in possession of information which allows them to manipulate the physical being of patients. It is the union of medical knowledge and the authority to use it with which physicians identify. Physicians are now partners with insurance companies not patients.

The notion supported by patients that physicians are in a position of authority above and separate from patients gives rise to the physician mystique. An interesting thing happened in the nineteen eighties between patients and their doctors. Patients began to be more aware the healthcare expertise they were being sold was not necessarily expert or healthful. As the dissatisfaction with their doctors grew, the interest in how patients could evaluate their own healing gained in popularity. Doctors responded. It suddenly became fashionable for physicians to admit to their patients that there were some things they didn't know. This was received by patients as being very progressive on the part of physicians. Everywhere doctors were saying "I don't know" and endearing themselves to their patients. It may be that the admission from doctors that they didn't know everything after pretending they did for so many decades was a fresh approach. It was a subtle shift away from omnipotence to admitting that possibly doctors cannot live up to the image they have created for themselves. It was also good for business. The problem is however, many physicians don't know what it is they don't understand. When doctors say they do not understand something it should not be a comfort to patients. It is notice to patients they must become more active in directing their own care.

Physicians think within a rigidly circumscribed physically based framework. The data from which they form medical decisions is founded on the science of the day. When people turn to physicians, they expect them to know all of the medical facts and how to use them for their own special benefit. Conflicts arise however, when physicians apply facts to human beings who are much more than a combination of physiological circumstances. Compounding the problem are physicians who rely heavily on others to interpret the facts for them. Generally, there are two types of physicians. Those who think for themselves and those who rely on others to diagnose for them. Some doctors treating a patient for the first time will read patient records and defer to the impressions and or diagnosis made by another doctor. It is up to patients to decide if it is appropriate for their physician to make up his own mind or accept another physician's assessment of their condition.

If the patient has seen his own physician about the same problem with no progress it is imperative to find someone who will investigate on his own. That may mean not transferring your old records to a new physician. The issue of whether or not to transfer records becomes important when the opinions contained in your chart are inaccurate. Doctors and nurses also categorize patients according to personality. Part of the contents of medical records are the personal and subjective impressions doctors have of their patients. It is unfortunate if those impressions are inaccurate or negative, because records will indicate it. Physicians are very defensive about what they do, and are usually surprised when patients openly disagree with them. Therefore, when patients differ with doctors and insist on fair treatment they may be labeled "difficult", and those who refuse treatment that they don't want are "non-compliant". Patients who find their doctors to be rude, arrogant or disrespectful and are assertive enough to let them know are also labeled in very unflattering terms. It is an important issue for two reasons. This type of designation is demeaning and creates frustration for patients. It also engenders apathy in patients for their prescribed treatment regime. Patients who insist they are ill when doctors say they are not become seen as people who are crying wolf. When this happens patients will withhold further problems from their doctor to avoid ridicule. This becomes a situation where patients may be actually hurting themselves in an attempt to avoid being frustrated by their doctor. The second is that it can actually interfere with subsequent treatment. It does this by predisposing a physician to relate to his patient in a negative way, based on what are the usually erroneous impressions of others. Physicians pass these conclusions about their patients on to other doctors via chart notes. The situation then repeats itself when patients seek out new doctors for help. Consider the patient who complained of leg pain and sought help from primary care and orthopedic specialists. Many months passed as he went from doctor to doctor never getting a diagnosis or relief from pain. What he did get was a reputation for being a malingerer who had invented his problem to get attention. Doctors were unable to placate him or convince him there was nothing wrong with his leg. At his insistence he was admitted to the hospital for exploratory surgery. Prior to surgery his physician resorted to ordering placebos to be given whenever he complained of pain. The nurses were instructed to tell him he was getting morphine. The patient remained in a great deal of pain right up to the time of surgery. In the operating room doctors found a benign tumor the size of a large orange in his leg which was responsible for his pain.

Errors that clinicians make are not entered into the official records. Mistakes (even the most obvious) are excluded from the chart material because of the possibility of malpractice lawsuits. Chart notes are always slanted advantageously toward providers, and perceptions can alter the accuracy of record keeping. Healthcare workers are taught that whatever they put into the chart must stand up to scrutiny in a court of law. Therefore, what physicians describe is not necessarily consistent with their patient's recall. Discrepancies about the details of what actually transpires between patient and physician may be resolved by altering the record to flatter to physician. Consider the patient who was discharged from the hospital and became very ill after returning home. The patient should have been given a prescription for prednisone which is a powerful immune system suppressant at discharge. But this was overlooked by the physician responsible for sending him home from the hospital. His condition worsened as a result of not having the medication he needed. He began having a great deal of pain. He phoned his doctor's office for help and was told there was nothing more to be done. He continued to call over the next few weeks to explain his worsening condition but to no avail. He was not told that he should have been given medication at the time of his discharge. At this point his physician accused him of making his problem worse by not taking his medication. When he informed his doctor he had been given no such prescription the mistake was realized. The physician had written in the chart that he gave his patient the medication. The chart reflected what should have happened, not what really happened. That is the essence and hidden problem of medical record keeping. What would seem to be a simple oversight easily remedied created a great deal of misery for this patient. He had two problems, one physical and one emotional. Not only was he medically neglected but at the same time he was insulted and treated very badly by his physician and staff. Small problems for doctors always have more serious implications for patients.

The patient chart is made up of two types of information. The first is data acquired as a result of medical testing, lab reports, x-rays, scans etc. As well as data created by personnel making objective observations. This includes vital signs, various monitoring equipment and the administration of medications. This information is composed without the interjection of subjective personal opinion. Second category data include personal impressions about the patient. There is a small area of overlap such as with X-ray interpretation, because the X-ray is an objective picture subjectively interpreted. It is important to remember that what the radiologist concludes about what he sees is his opinion. It is not uncommon to have very different readings of the same x-ray film by two different doctors. (Neither does it guarantee a correct interpretation just because a radiologist versus a non-specialist evaluates the x-ray.) Whatever is subject to interpretation is also subject to misinterpretation. There are other situations which combine subjective and objective data so it is wise to review your own records when you can. Patients should always be aware of what is contained in their records even if they are not having urgent problems. The laws applied to medical records may vary slightly from state to state regarding access. There is also a strong movement underway to block patients from obtaining them. But most patients will be successful in getting their records if they are persistent.

After deciding you want to transfer medical records to another physician or specialist, you must also decide which records to transfer. Doctors can tell you (and most do) what to send but you must actually authorize moving your records. You may also find that physicians have transferred your records without your permission. They may ask you to give them authorization later. This is done to obscure the fact that they were transferred without authorization. You are not obligated to sign a back-dated authorization. Also, keep in mind that records are frequently lost in the transfer from place to place. So if you will be traveling long distances or need them transferred quickly you should hand carry them. Doctors and records departments may try to discourage you from carrying your own records. This is usually a holdover from the days when patients were not allowed to know what was in their records. Ignore their protestations and demand to hand carry your records if and when you need to.

If there is something in the record you don't want transferred you can edit your records. The original documentation is required to stay where it originated. But copies can be edited and certain items removed as you choose. Some medical records departments will go to great lengths to make it difficult for you to examine or copy your records. This is usually because a) it makes more work for them b) they themselves do not understand the rights you have regarding your records c) they think you are incapable of understanding what is in your records and therefore must protect you from what you will misinterpret d) they have something to hide e) they have been lost.

If you believe that your records have inaccuracies or poorly formed opinions you may choose to exclude them from what you transfer. If there is a charge for the transfer of records you may wish to send along only lab work, scans etc. It is the responsibility of the physician to determine if he has sufficient information to make an accurate diagnosis. If there are test results he needs, he may feel what has already been done is sufficient. It may also be appropriate to redo tests, you should remember that it is not carved in stone that all your records should be transferred. The way to a diagnosis can take several different routes. It is a patient's right to transfer his records. It is the privilege of the physician to ask the patient to authorize the transfer.

Some physicians are very good a making the right diagnosis. But there those who are not so skilled at it. Diagnosis is the art of detection using medical knowledge. That means knowing where and how to look for answers. The ability to think creatively within a diagnostic framework is necessary. It also requires the talent to listen to patients and understand what is important to the patient. Skillful interpretation of what the patient says combined with the clinical data is a must. There are some physicians who don't cultivate the right type of thinking necessary to arrive at the right diagnosis. Even when a patient goes to a physician for the exclusive purpose of a new or second opinion that doesn't necessarily mean the doctor will do his own thinking. The ability to be discerning and perceptive doesn't automatically come with a medical degree. Nor is astute medical thought restricted to physicians. Many patients go physicians for confirmation about what they think their problem is. And many patients are right. When a physician becomes stymied he should see that his patient finds someone else who can help. Some will not make the proper referrals because of their own ego. In that case the patient has been done a serious disservice. This may be true even if the patient has been referred from a family practice office to a specialist for an in-depth look at a problem. A difficult diagnosis requires persistence and patience from consumers. Some doctors will expend more effort for patients they like or find especially interesting. Two patients with like diagnosis and treatment may receive a different quality of care from the same physician. Doctors have favorite patients just as they have patients they don't like. Most physicians try to be impartial but when it doesn't happen, the personality of either patient or physician can have a powerful negative influence on treatment. An atmosphere of antagonism between doctor and patient decreases what should be a highly motivated search for the answer to the patient's problem.

Another important factor to be aware of is that physicians will usually prescribe the most common treatment for patient problems. But the most common answer to a problem may not be the correct one. A doctor who does not invest enough thought in the diagnostic process in the beginning may delay the correct diagnosis while the patient continues to suffer and be compromised. As we all know, undue delay in treatment may have very serious consequences. Today, insurance companies may not pay for the time and expense required to make the all important diagnosis. Some may even penalize doctors for ordering the appropriate tests. This only encourages doctors to justify a sloppy job of investigation.

In his book "Lethal Medicine" Harvey Wachsman MD.JD. provides a quote from Cecil's Textbook of Medicine that cautions:

> "Too often previous examinations are accepted in lieu of a fresh, independent look to the patient's detriment. A detailed chronological development of all the symptomatology must be undertaken with care, and the patient's observations must not be dismissed because they do not happen to fit the pattern of a disease process the physician is entertaining. What a patient says is to be believed and to be understood to the best of the physicians ability."

The current knowledge of physiology, pharmaceutics, and rigid parameters set by physicians and their attorneys define the context within which diagnosis happens. And now HMOs and insurance companies have added their restrictions. So what exists are several sub-systems that manage healthcare operations for their own gain. The system is to be benefited before the patient is allowed to benefit. For healthcare to really be health care the consumer must be elevated to the status of his real being, over and above dry impersonal facts and self-serving regulations. In the same way, individuals employed in healthcare mark their place in the system with the their own personal priorities. Whether one undertakes to examine the issue of health by looking at the system or by the role of the individual in it, the results are the same. Patients are not the highest priority.

It is often the physician's view that patient fees should reimburse him for the costs of his training. This peculiar idea that consumers owe physicians for the financial burden they assumed in financing their education is fostered by physicians. For doctors, the personal problems they may have had to overcome to finish school justify exorbitant fee structures. If there is a debt to repay it is to the consumer who provides physicians with an opportunity to earn a living doing what they have been taught to do. But patients actually have no moral or ethical obligation to repay physicians for the costs of their training.

It can be worthwhile to ask the office staff how long your physician has maintained his own private practice. There are very good reasons for using a physician who is new and there are also good reasons for not choosing one. Some physicians are more temperamentally suited to taking on new challenges. Whatever self doubts people in general may have doctors are subject to as well. But in this instance it is your life on the line not theirs. Insecurity takes different forms and most patients are not aware of how insecure their doctors can be. Two factors that contribute to the unease of new physicians are a) the level of their own self confidence and medical expertise b) what their peer group may think of their judgment. These things may not necessarily translate into poor patient care. When they do it can involve too much care in the form of unnecessary treatment. To be sure treatment is going to work some physicians prescribe more medical therapy than is actually required. Impatience to see results can come from a need to reassure themselves that they have chosen the right treatment. But treatment takes time, and it is going to take as much time as required to effect a cure. Rushing therapy to its conclusion is not necessary.

The other side of the coin gives us doctors who don't take action when they should. Sometimes people just starting out are slow to act from simple timidity. Fear of doing the wrong thing can lead to doing nothing at all. Physicians fear their own inadequacies and what that may mean for their patients. Criticism from their peers is largely an irrational fear doctors have. In spite of this, fear may be a higher priority than the patient. Physicians rarely censure other doctors even for the most egregious and flagrant malpractice. But fear is a dominant motivation for physicians today. To vary from routine treatment (even though it is medically sound and helpful to the patient) can cause a physician to withhold it. If treatment causes a doctor to stand out even in a minor way, the patient may suffer for it. Doctors like these who "go along to get along" are cowardly but not uncommon.

Physicians and others in the healthcare field seek to make patients and their problems conform to the routine. Pigeon-holing patients is comforting to the insecure because they can then give them textbook treatment. To see patients as individuals is more time consuming. It means more factors to consider and more questions to answer. When management groups limit a doctor's time to eight minutes per patient a standard limit, this is one result. Unfortunately, patients must bear the consequences of such faulty thinking. No two patients are alike and people must be considered as individuals before they are seen as patients. In most instances a treatment protocol treatment allows for the opportunity to tailor treatment to specific patient need and desire. When physicians fail to do that it can indicate a fearful or selfish nature. These attitudes are obvious to patients and make them feel as though their needs are not important. Provider produced stress experienced by patients in these situations is frustrating and does not encourage patients to accept treatment plans.

On the positive side, doctors just coming into practice may be more aware of and more comfortable with newer treatment options. Doctors from a progressive hospital training program may have a fresh perspective which can aid both diagnosis and long term care. What determines the direction physicians take is dictated by training but just as certainly by their various personalities. Qualities of intellect, reason, and confidence will ultimately decide how a physician responds to the demands of private practice.

The American public is being oversold on the cures our healthcare system purports to be capable of. Expensive technology and people qualified to use it have a carefully crafted image that they cannot possibly live up to. At the same time we are denied access to what they claim to provide by insurance companies and HMOs. The left hand extends healthcare to us while the right prevents us from taking it. The last ten years have made it clear just how difficult it can be to get good healthcare. Added to that disillusionment is the realization that people are not getting what they believe they have paid for.

When one looks at the advertising of healthcare two things stand out. The first and foremost is the image of a provider group that practices the art of medicine in a compassionate, pristine environment. Second, that the normal characteristics of the human body are being exaggerated and made to seem abnormal. Products and the problems they fix have been blown way out of proportion, dry skin no longer requires lotion but dry skin medicine as though simple dry skin is a serious pathological condition.

This type of advertising puts added pressure on physicians to deliver what they cannot. But it also creates an expectation in the minds of the public that they are safer than they really are. It is a business selling inflated images. One aspect of such spin is when doctors suggest the use of newer procedures or medicines to patients. The public is conditioned to believe that "new" is better. It is touted in ads on TV and in magazines. No one will argue that many new procedures are improvements over the old. But a physician must develop skill with a new technique before he advocates its use. And there are risks to every treatment. Experience is key to the safe use of any procedure or medical therapy. Consumers can be easily persuaded to accept a new treatment by their physicians. Therefore, it is up to the physician to be fair when representing the known risks and benefits. Physicians are compelled (for legal reasons) to do this in written form for their patients. Patients are then bombarded with technical language, strange statistics and incoherent paperwork on consent forms. These consents do very little to give patients practical, usable information. Their real purpose is for use in the courtroom to provide malpractice protection for physicians. The patient must depend on the physician (who else?) to introduce the idea of a new treatment, and present its risks in understandable terms. In the end it is up to the physician and his interpretation of value vs. risk that the patient must rely on. Consumers are told to trust in the safety of treatment. Combine the idea of safety together with a physician's enthusiasm for a new medicine or surgery and any hesitancy on the part of the patient is quickly dispelled. Unfortunately, some physicians can get carried away with new ideas and use them on patients too soon. They transmit the assurance of expertise to their patients before they are truly proficient. The training for physicians using new methods often is not as uniform or thorough as it should be. The result is a wide range of skill levels. Consumers should not undertake a new procedure until they are satisfied in their own mind that their physician is good at using it. Always ask your physician:

How long has this procedure been used?

What are the risks for me in my particular situation?

How many times have you personally performed it?

What types of problems have you had using it?

Would you encourage a member of your family to use it?

You must consider carefully how much personal experience your physician has. A few doctors will encourage patients to try something new so they (your doctor) can gain experience with it. Some will simply misjudge their own abilities. There is pressure on patients to accept new treatments from their physicians, and pressure on physicians to perform new procedures from their peers. Outside pressure from manufacturers who want to sell products add to the confusion. It is also very important for patients to understand what the long term effects of procedures will be. Consumers must assume a position based on a balanced view of possible treatment. Doctors should restrict their thinking to only those things that are of benefit to their patients. When those viewpoints coincide the correct decision about treatment can be made. The majority of doctors perform safely and use new procedures that they feel will be truly beneficial. But the few who succumb to their own ego and outside pressures can do great harm. Just as extreme skiers plunge down dangerous mountain slopes for the thrill of it, physicians may experience medicine as adventure. Pushing the profession of medicine into new territories can be exciting when it works. Unfortunately extreme medicine has left more than one patient in extremes.

The old Irish chieftains used to send their servants into battle first to spare themselves unknown dangers. These gallowglass soldiers were sacrificed for their masters. Without careful consideration of all options and potentialities patients may find that they too can relate to the unfortunate gallowglass.

Medicine is antagonistic to the natural state of man. Practitioners have made its practice an adversarial one between patient and practitioner. It is in medicine's nature to do violence in the attempt to effect a cure. Violence may come in the form of routine therapy or more drastic measures such as surgery. However it appears, or the rationale behind it, treatment is not the benign entity physicians consider it to be. Even when some of the misery it causes are acknowledged doctors, they believe it to be right, reasonable and secondary to their purpose. Human beings are not designed to accept unnatural methods to restore their natural condition. The physician asserts the superiority of his system as he denies nature's authority. If physicians cannot change therapy they can and must change their perspective to one of protection and support for patients. This means protecting patients from therapy when necessary. Physicians are asking patients to defer their belief system (or at the very least keep it to themselves) during treatment.

The greatest challenge to physicians today is learning to practice without paying attention to their conscience. Finding a way to work in the system to provide proper care to patients while the system is reducing that care is the physician's paradox. Some will convince themselves that managed care is actually a good thing for patients. Others who are near the end of their career retire, pushed out by their own disgust at what is happening. For those who are new to the practice of medicine and know no other system the abdication of caring is easier. In time, these physicians will become the hardest to work with because it will be their only operating frame of reference. Thus it is that physicians fulfill Nietzsche's characterization of the pale criminal - one who has the courage of the knife but not the blood. Medicine lives on misery, its life blood is the blood of its patients. Clinicians launder their own psyche by transforming the long-suffering of patients into clinical data. Thus exists the pale criminal, who soothes his own suffering with professional and social rewards. Preferring to assign blame for its failures on patients, managed care, and politics. The Wall Street Journal addresses this in an article that appeared on 12-22-97. Discussing the furor over recently prescribed new drugs for weight loss the article reports; In the fallout, doctors are under attack for prescribing the pills too much, too readily and to the wrong patients-the same criticism they faced concerning antibiotics and hyperactive therapies. Doctors say it isn't all their fault, and they cite a contributing factor: pushy patients. Prodded by an explosion in direct to customer-to-customer advertising of prescription drugs, patients press their physicians for quick treatments for everything from flu symptoms to unsightly toenails....Patients wheedled, begged and berated to get doctors to prescribe the weight-loss drugs, doctors say. Some physicians set up clinics specializing in diet pills and advertised heavily, making it even harder on doctors who had reservations. "If a consumer is making enough noise, it can overcome a physician's objections" says Thomas Hirsch, an internist at Dean Medical Center, Madison, Wis." The feeble rationalization that doctors are incapable of saying no to patients when they request inappropriate medications is only one more example of doctors blaming patients for their mistakes. The article continues: If doctors don't like patients asking about advertised drugs, "I say too bad to the doctors," says Lawrence Weber, an asthma and allergy sufferer and head of Weber Public Relations Worldwide (which doesn't have drug-company clients) "I think its good that a patient read and be informed, even if its from an ad. Doctors are going to have to live with a far more informed patient." ... In the end, though, prescribing decisions are the doctor's responsibility. "There's no detail man or pharmaceutical company or patient that puts a gun to a doctor's head to write a prescription," says Jerry Avorn, associate professor at Harvard Medical School. "Ultimately, it isn't the patient's name on the prescription, it's the doctor's." Patients are increasingly being put in no-win situations by doctors. As pressures on doctors mount they shift their inability to cope onto patients. Defensive medicine is an imperative today-for the patient.

Akin to placing blame on patients is the newest and most insidious form of the abuse excuse. According to the Christian Science Monitor: American workers took home a poor report-card in a recent survey of 4,500 companies by NAM (National Association of Manufacturers in Washington)

- 60 percent say their workers lack basic math skills

- 55 percent find their workers are seriously weak in basic writing and comprehension skills

- 63 percent say their workers are tardy, chronically absent, or unwilling to work a full day.

- Half found it difficult to give employees more autonomy.

- Two-thirds have difficulty improving productivity and upgrading technology.

Poorly trained workers with inadequate communication skills produce employees who either can't or won't think about what they are doing. When that factor coincides with a person placed in a limited power situation the result is a worker whose ego is much larger than their functionality. Workers are blaming their own bad behavior on patients, calling them abusive when they are in actuality not abusive. Employees invite censure through thoughtlessness, mistakes, and their own abusive behaviors. When patients dare to speak the truth and reflect back to workers what they have done the worker responds by calling by labeling the patient abusive. Recording and spreading the word that a certain patient is abusive they have absolved themselves of their wretched or inadequate response to a situation. They have also cut the patient off from getting the situation corrected. Patients called abusive are instantly dismissed as not having legitimate complaints. Workers who deliberately misinform doctors and other staff about patients usually do so to cover up their own behavior. Nothing rankles a staff member more than being recognized by the patient as incompetent. At a time when I was seriously ill and needed to be admitted to the hospital I requested a private room and was told there was nothing available.

I knew this to be untrue because this was a hospital that was rarely filled to capacity and had many private rooms. Because of a compromised immune system I refused to be placed into a ward where the exposure to infectious agent would be multiplied. The nurse countered with "there are no private rooms available on the floor that the doctor has requested." This too was an ignorant argument because no doctor will turn a patient with a potentially fatal problem because of a bed assignment. In addition to which this hospital places medical patients on a variety of different floors. But by this time the nurses had too much ego invested in the situation to back down. They refused to back down and I wouldn't compromise my health situation by accepting an ego based decision that could prove harmful to me. My requests to speak to the doctor, supervisor and admitting department were all denied by these emergency nurses. Their opinions of themselves being so high and their opinion of me as weak and ignorant made them over confident. I had only one recourse left and I took it. I left the hospital came home and called the admitting department myself. I asked if the ER had put in my request for a private room anywhere in the hospital and they replied no, they hadn't. But she did say that the ER nurses had been there immediately after I left to inquire about the availability of private rooms in the hospital. Anxious about having called my bluff they were worried about how to cover themselves if having turned me away they had put themselves in jeopardy! I asked about the availability of a private room on a floor that took medical patients routinely and was told there were six. There were also other floors who could have accepted a private medical patient temporarily. She asked me which room I would like, I told her and was assigned the room . I went back to the hospital and was admitted to a private room. In another instance I was assigned to a floor with all double bed rooms. However there were many rooms with no patients at all. I asked the nurse to please not put another patient in the room with me and note it on the chart. On this particular night I was told there were only approximately four to five patients. The likelihood that so many patients would be admitted to fill up all beds was extremely remote at best. Still, the staff refused to honor my request. To ensure privacy I had to move to from the relatively less expensive floor to a much more expensive one.

In both of these situations doctors, nurses, and other staff were informed orally and in written form that I was uncooperative, demanding and refusing to comply with care. All of this character assassination was completed before I had seen my doctor or received any care whatsoever. As soon as the paperwork is initiated the slurs against patients recorded to put the patient in a bad light and shield staff from well deserved criticism. Staff needs are always first, and if that means discrediting patients at the onset that's how it will be.

This illustrates the patient's paradox. I do not necessarily recommend leaving the hospital when your physician wants you to stay. But what does the patient do when he feels he may be worse off if he does. Hospitals are paid to provide a safe environment. But that is not the reality of today. Often the choice for patients is, which is safer to be ill inside a hospital or out of one. Providers have stuck their head in the sand and deny the fears of consumers. But those fears are real and many are based on personal experience.

Physicians have their own paradox to deal with. Do they perform with their patients as a priority or do they comply with a system that allows room for individualized treatment? System compliance or improved patient care? Should physicians work to suppress their conscience or risk working around the system. How much can physicians actually do to improve the lot of their patients? Individually they can begin to believe in patients and their way of looking at the world. The practice of medicine should start with the patient, not the corporate structure. Collectively, physicians must assert patient rights, working to change the structure of medical care delivery. The earnest physician has only one priority, his patient. If laws have to change they can make it happen. If standards of care need to be raised they can do it. The biggest obstacle facing physicians is learning to practice within the managed care structure without a conscience. Knowing that they cannot provide care based on patient need must somehow be justified in their own mind. Physicians are instruments of an often damaging and cruel system. Finding a way to ply their trade without confronting the trauma it causes is a formidable task. However, the conscience that has been compromised reflects the predominant thought today and therefor is supported. As some physicians learn to rationalize and decrease their own discomfort they become more uncomfortable in the presence of others who don't. Physicians cannot work to treat pain and suffering at the same time they are learning to deny its existence. The hard heart is always uncomfortable in the presence of the heart that is touched by suffering. The elaborate philosophical, psychological analysis of patients is more reflective of intellectual sophistry than it is an honest appraisal of the patient condition today. "This peoples heart is waxed gross, and their eyes are dull of hearing, and their eyes are closed;" Book of Matthew, English Revised Bible.

Managed care is the Rubicon of American healthcare. The medical profession has made its decision to accept managed care and make it their choice of economic sustenance.

Having made this irrevocable decision their future course is set. Consumers must not make the same decision. To do so will condemn the future of medicine to its past. Consumers choosing to use the healthcare system without accepting the premise upon which it is founded. Consumers must view healthcare not as a service but a product. Inferior products and those that sell them must be made to be accountable for the damage caused by both the product and those who use it. For medicine this is a time of business. Let consumers demand their money's worth in goods and services. Let physicians prove their worth, and answer to patients not the protective medical boards which watch over them, keeping them secure even when grossly incompetent. Patient mentality must change to that of one which has zero tolerance for incompetence, physical and emotional abuse. It is the consumers place to sit on each and every board that sets medical standards and judges the actions of physicians. Physicians do far too damage to be allowed to govern themselves. The fox has been guarding the hen house far too long. Let those who must subject themselves to the system govern the system. If patients are part of the system it is they who must judge the system. Consumers must represent themselves in the design and evaluation of every aspect of care. No one knows more about whether the influence of the system is healthful than the patient. The patient is the expert.

We don't have a system that will profit by a list of things patients can do to improve their care. The superficial application of tips to "empower patients" and pop psychology. A quickie how to manual won't suffice. Telling patients to research the credentials of their doctors while nice won't solve the deep problems. Telling doctors to listen more carefully to patients and attend to the thought patients have about that care can't provide much help. That is why patients are increasingly frustrated and the future of the system not optimistic but dismal and dark.

Chapter 3

Office To Hospital - Health And Hazards

"In trying to cure one old disease, we give rise to a hundred new ones."
Mahatma Gandhi

The office experience is a little like stepping into quicksand. The more you struggle against it the more dangerous it becomes. Far from becoming a source of relief for suffering it has evolved into the starting point for the necessary practice of defensive medicine by consumers. The current office milieu is one of complexity and escalating danger to patients. As corporate profits rise it encourages insurance companies and HMO's to further restrict not only access to care but care itself after entry into the system is won. The first roadblock to what patients need is the doctors office.

The single biggest obstacle to getting good care from a physician's office is the application of arbitrary policies which serve to include some patients and exclude others. Physicians and their staff operate from a negative orientation out of which must come something positive - good healthcare - for their patients. Both insurance and the typical HMO structure serve as triage bodies, not to provide care on the basis of need but ability to pay. Our healthcare system manages itself more like a private club that chooses who it will admit or dismiss. This mind-set is enough to smother even the most noble and caring motivations of practitioners. The day to day maneuvering of the system is further compromised by many healthcare workers who are not suited to public service and are poorly trained.

Practitioners who don't know how to relate to healthy, human beings are hopeless as well as helpless when called upon to assist patients who are in a compromised state of health. In spite of this some doctors offices are populated with people who simply should not be allowed to work in them. This requires consumers to be aware of not only what is in their best interest but simultaneously to defend themselves against what may be injurious. Offices designed to turn a profit will do just that. Offices which are dedicated to the welfare of patients before profit will find their way full of corporate obstacles.

Refined technology comes with a high price tag. Of what possible use can healthcare be if patients especially those in urgent need, find care to be inaccessible.

It is better to learn the intimate details of the office situation without the trauma of first hand experience. Unfortunately offices will present themselves in light of the ideal of care delivery rather than the reality of what goes on in an office setting. Thus it is that going to the doctor's office becomes an adventure itself. Office care has improvement potential. However, change initiated without patient guidance will surely fail. Negotiating their way through the system is more than many ill people can cope with. Nor do practitioners cope with it well. Your healthcare begins when you pick up the phone to make an appointment with your doctor. How the staff handles your call can be an indication of way the entire office process will be managed. The front office staff is that group of people who make appointments, transfer records, relay messages from patients to doctors and coordinate appointments for patients with laboratories, X-rays and other patient services.

Contrary to popular understanding, for the office staff not making appointments for patients is just as important as making them. Putting too many patients on the schedule is something to be avoided, even when patients have a legitimate need to be seen. The first priority is managing the flow of patients through the office. When schedule management is the goal patients automatically become a secondary consideration. Managing a medical office can be less about patient care than efficiency. Most offices are organized and staffed by office managers, clerical staff and people processing insurance claims. In practical terms the physician is removed (by his own choosing) from the daily operations of his office. Usually, there is more staff dedicated to clerical work than actual patient care. Today there is a clear shift away from serving patients to supporting the practice as a business enterprise devoted first to itself. Patient need is re-shaped by and must conform to a smooth running office. Before a patient has entered the office his needs have already been subordinated. Smaller practices have been much more successful at keeping patients as a priority, and a few larger office groups have tried to resist changes forced on them by a profit driven healthcare industry. But most offices have evolved into something consumers have difficulty understanding or relating to.

Having qualified people employed in doctors offices is important for several reasons. Consumers shouldn't need to even consider whether or not personnel are qualified. But with new standards of care now in place it is a very real concern. The first is that appointments for patients are made by office staff not the physician. The need for urgent, or involved appointments requiring extra time is determined by non-medical personnel. The second is that the information conveyed to physicians about their patients by their staff must be accurate. Thirdly, and perhaps most importantly consumers rely on what they believe to be office staff expertise. Consumers should be able to count on staff to be competent enough to think through and understand what the implications of their actions will be. By downgrading the qualifications for office personnel the ability of staff to discern potentially serious situations from routine ones is being lost. Triage of patient need is a skill that is vital to an office where a large volume of patients are seen in a day. But triage must be taught and it is something that is not given enough emphasis in offices.

There are two forms of triage, the first is based on the degree of urgency. The most seriously ill are seen first. But a new form of triage has come into being as a result of managed care. Now the sickest are put off or denied appointments altogether. Because the very ill may require more time than the standard office time limit on visits these patients are shuffled off to expensive emergency rooms. But once there these patients will get only "band-aid" treatment until they can get an appointment with their own doctor. Thus patients may have to go to the ER more than once before they can get an office appointment. Ironically, when a very ill patient is seen in the office it may not take more time because the physician is more familiar with this type of patient. Additionally, the care the patient gets in the ER may be lacking due to a lack of medical records, medical history and current treatment regime. The typical office staff consists of:

Receptionist - to make appointments and manage the patient flow through the office. He may have training in medical terminology but not patient care.

Medical office assistant (MOA) - These people take patients back to the examining room and make them ready for the doctor. MOAs (as they may be called) are trained only in the basics of office care. They may have some medical terminology training and know how to take patient vital signs - blood pressure, temperature, etcetera. The length of their training is some number of weeks at technical schools or community colleges. It is important to remember that simply taking a blood pressure is quite different from understanding what blood pressure is. When asking questions remember that an MOA does not have the training to offer a medical opinion or advice.

Certified nursing assistant (CNA) - CNAs are similar in training to MOAs but may have more practical background in assisting patients with care in the hospital or home, dressing, bathing, bandaging etc. The length of training may be several weeks to a few months.

Licensed practical nurses (LPN) or licensed vocational nurses (LVN) - LPNs or LVNs have a more extensive education than office assistants. The length of their training is usually under two years in a nursing school, or college setting. There the emphasis is on caring for patients in hospitals or skilled nursing facilities where observation and bedside care are stressed. Dressing changes, nutrition, monitoring and administering IV therapy, injections, and using a wide variety of equipment are included in training. Most LPNs tend to be proficient at these tasks. Because doctors offices and outpatient clinics are doing more procedures that hospitals used to do practical nurses can be a major asset for patients in the office.

Registered nurses - Training time for RNs varies from two to four years. Most RNs graduating today have either associate or baccalaureate degrees. Three year diploma schools which were the standard for many years and graduated many skilled nurses are being phased out. Regardless of diploma or degree RNs share a body of knowledge with more thorough training in physiological assessment, and the needs of patients in hospitals and community health situations. RNs have a broader scope of clinical expertise than those with less training time. Their education emphasizes more sophisticated technological skill with care plan formulation and implementation. Both LPNs and RNs must pass state examinations before they are granted a license to practice.

Most patients are unaware of the different qualifications for office staff and don't realize that it is important. The receptionist will defer to the "nurse" when taking messages from patients to doctors and for questions about patient problems. But white lab coats and unfamiliar initials on name tags give patients mistaken impressions of authority.

Licensed nurses are being phased out of doctors offices at a rapid rate and office assistants are assuming the role of licensed nurses. The result is that people are doing tasks and making decisions that they are too inexperienced or unqualified to make. That is dangerous because patients are arriving at doctor's offices with increasingly complex problems. As patient situations become more difficult to assess, the training to care for these patients should increase not decrease. The underlying cause for turning to untrained and marginally qualified people in doctors offices is the same as it is in any business; to cut cost and increase profit. Insurance companies and HMOs are demanding that patient care be reduced to save money and doctors who are affiliated with some of these corporations have lost the authority to make staffing decisions. Others simply do not want to pay the higher wages and benefits professional nurses deserve. Doctors defend these cost cutting measures by saying for instance, that a licensed nurse is not needed simply to usher a patient back to an exam room and take a blood pressure. Unfortunately, office assistants are usually expected to do much more.

Doctors do not want to be slowed down by patient problems happening out of the office. But problems with patients do occur outside the office. These issues are then referred to the office assistant or "nurse" as they are referred to. Anyone who is called "nurse" should in fact be a real nurse. All messages and problems are evaluated for importance and urgency by the assistant first. This means that before a problem of yours can be "presented" to the doctor for his advice the assistant interprets the situation for him. She decides if the problem is important enough to warrant the doctor's personal attention. If the problem is something that he does need to know about in her opinion, she condenses it and then passes it along. Physicians have always relied very heavily on the impressions of staff when dealing with phone messages. As the quality of personnel training decreases, the issue becomes a bigger issue of trust. Is an assistant really qualified to understand and convey your problem to the doctor? Do you want someone with more or less training? Medical problems should only be evaluated by people with medical training, not someone whose priority is manipulating a schedule. As medicine continues to advances proper diagnosis and intervention depend on the ability to recognize increasingly subtle signs and symptoms. As it is now, someone with rudimentary skill is evaluating what may be complex symptoms.

When that happens important things can get missed. It is unfair to staff to expect them to function beyond their level of skill. But it is even more important to the patient when assistants confuse symptoms of indigestion with a heart attack. If the symptoms of something so important can get missed or confused (and they do) think how many other types of patient situations are vulnerable to mistakes. When you factor in medication problems, and the handling of medical records necessary to make a safe assessment of patient concerns, this becomes a very important issue.

How many people do you know who have tried desperately to convey to the office nurse the importance of a problem and not been taken seriously? Or, how many people have been told they don't have a problem only to find themselves with major problems later that could and should have been avoided. These are daily events that are increasing as doctors have less time than ever before to spend with patients. Health maintenance organizations and other corporate groups can control the volume of patients that go through doctors offices in a single day. Many doctors are being forced to see more patients in a day than they can adequately evaluate and respond to. In some instances these corporations will not allow a physician to "close" his practice to new patients even when it becomes impossible to care for already established patients due to lack of time. It takes time to listen to patients and review medical reports, and there is no substitute for lost time. When time-per-patient shrinks, patient care is diminished. Also, as consumers are deprived of the ability to choose their own physicians they are forced into offices where the practice of medicine is becoming unsafe. When the control of something so basic as how large a practice can become is taken away from the physician, will lead to more and bigger problems. If care begins badly it can be very difficult to get back on track later. If there isn't time to do it right in the beginning there won't be more time later. The time in between making an appointment and actually getting in to see the doctor is lengthening, even more so for a visit with a specialist. The longer patients wait for treatment the more harm may accrue. Doctors get locked into situations that even they recognize as potentially detrimental and consumers are trapped into frustrating situations they cannot influence. The higher the potential for profit climbs the more rigidly controlled the people caught in the system are.

Outside business controls on a medical practice are so demanding, it makes it even more important to have only the most astute people working in doctors offices. It takes people with good technical, observational and communication skills to help consumers through a system so heavily weighted against patients by big business. Cost cutting is the primary objective in the commerce of healthcare. There is no job in an office that isn't important but when qualified people are hired they are rarely adequately compensated. A medical practice pays big dividends, but the boon goes to corporations. For nurses the average pay rate is significantly lower in the office than in hospitals and other places of employment. Many nurses come to office jobs with the expectation they won't have to work as hard in an office as they would in the hospital. They trade physically harder hospital work with more pay for office work with better hours and less physical labor. That doesn't seem remarkable until you realize that what doctors offices need is people willing to work harder for patients not someone whose mindset is about less work. Failure to give workers ongoing education to improve their job skills is a problem for healthcare workers as much as it is for patients. Dual factors of little training and low pay contribute to the idea that office workers and their jobs are not so crucial as hospital work. But to patients who need care how everyone in the office performs is important. Illness of any sort is stressful. To heal, people must focus on themselves and direct their energy in those ways that create a less difficult and more positive healing environment. That is something rarely (if ever) by appreciated by employees in the doctor's offices. Long delays in getting appointments, phone calls not returned, and rude or thoughtless behavior causes patients to direct energy away from themselves and replaces it with frustration and anxiety. For patients, a defensive posture is a must in crowded, impersonal offices. It has become the "job" of the patient to make sure mistakes are not being made. That decreases the available energy for cooperating with treatment plans. A long waiting time and a very short time spent with their doctors discourages patients. Office time should be an opportunity for patients to work with their physicians for better healing. Consumers are caught in a system where they feel they are without an advocate who will give their needs a high priority. Patients are using their attention to monitor and correct healthcare workers instead of healing. The elderly and very young are perhaps the most vulnerable but we are all at risk for the mistakes of healthcare workers. Even if consumers are better educated about how to protect themselves they may not be able to use what they learn in the throes of an illness. If they do manage to monitor their care intelligently they are left with the frustration of knowing they are forced to do a job that belongs to someone else. Consumers should always have control over their own care, but they should never be expected to do the job of professionals who aren't doing theirs.

Facilitating the best direct route for consumers trying to find their way through the healthcare system must revert back to the physicians who are ultimately responsible for their patients. The reputation a physician has with patients can be made or broken by his staff in the front office. When patients think back about their experience with a physician they also remember how they were treated by his staff.

The first impression of a doctor that a patient has is created by his front office staff and if that isn't favorable it leaves a strong negative imprint on patients. If someone in the front is inattentive and careless about setting up a chart for new patients on the first visit for instance, that same person may be just as careless phoning in a prescription for you. In one office I know the receptionist has a reputation for mishandling prescriptions; phoning them into the wrong pharmacy or mixing up names of patients and giving the wrong medicine to the wrong patient. In another office the nurse who calls in prescriptions has put off pharmacists so badly that the mere mention of the doctor's name evokes groans and complaints. These kinds of things may happen in the office of otherwise competent physicians who are unaware of what is going on at the front desk. Most clinicians are truly unaware of their reputation among both patients and other professionals. Doctors are busy with patients in exam rooms and do not have a complete picture of what is happening up front. They think they do of course. But what the physician knows about how his people are conducting themselves up front is what his staff want him to know. What they would like him to know is naturally, what a wonderful job they are doing. But when the behavior of the front office is not what it should be it makes a doctor look very foolish. Healthcare employees are a very defensive group. Some of the most bitter criticism I hear about doctors from patients can be traced back to the front office and the inappropriate behavior of his staff. If physicians had a true understanding of how important the front office is to their image and reputation, many people now in front offices no longer be there. Everyone in the front functions as a spin doctor at one time or another, reshaping situations to put themselves in the best possible light. Problems created for patients by staff are rarely acknowledged much less corrected by physicians.

However if a problem does come to his attention, you can be quite sure that when his staff and the patient disagree, staff will say what they must to make the patient out to be the cause of the problem. When difficulties arise it is important to tell your doctor about them yourself and avoid the inevitable "front office spin".

There will always be those situations which require emergency room visits, and many patients who should use the emergency room as their first contact. But to force patients into an emergency department unnecessarily does a grave disservice to hospitals and patients alike. Patients without the financial resources needed for the ER will go without care causing further harm, and others will incur a large debt only to told by the ER physician to contact his doctor's office instead. Doctors spend years enduring long hours and overwork training in crowded hospitals. When they set up an office of their own in the suburbs, they want a well organized, smooth running practice without making room for patients who need prompt care.

It doesn't take a Ph.D. to know you haven't been treated fairly. However, this fact seems to be lost on healthcare workers. Most believe that patients are not familiar enough with the intricacies of their jobs to distinguish between actual protocol and mere appearances. It is the insider (practitioner) versus the outsider (patient) mentality that creates this misconception. But patients are more astute at assessing the impact of staff action than the staff themselves. Patients think through a situation to its probable practical outcome with regard to cost, convenience and effect on family. What appear to staff to be small issues can be high priority items for many patients, particularly the disabled and elderly who must coordinate with others to facilitate their care. Employees are very task- oriented, not thinking ahead to the implications of their actions. Therefore, to workers it matters less how a task affects patients than getting the task done. It also means that priorities for healthcare workers are not the same as they are for consumers. It is not enough to tell patients what to do without knowing if it possible for them to follow through on treatment plans.

Consumers must conform their needs to fit the way the system wants to handle them. There is no room for accommodating patient need if that need interferes with the routine of an office. The "insider-outsider mentality" model says: for an office practice to serve patients in the best possible way, the office needs must be met first. It also says that if a difference of opinion exists between the two, the office way of doing things will prevail. As healthcare rushes into the next century it has become less cognizant of what is really required to produce a truly viable environment within which healing can happen. Offices are places of hard, dry soil, not the fertile ground needed to cultivate healing.

By putting themselves first, providers turn a blind eye to those ways of doing things that might improve things for office patients. One of the simplest and most glaring examples of the "provider first" attitude is the use of answering machines. This is a classic response illustrating how providers supply solutions to problems. The situation: too many patients too little time. As more people are pushed through offices it becomes more difficult to manage the flow due to a rising number of calls. Rather than hire an additional person or reassign tasks, offices prefer to install voice mail. For providers this creates an immediate resolution to problems caused by an increasingly heavy patient load. But for consumers it can be hazardous. What this solution tells patients trying to contact their doctor is that a) their call is not important enough to be answered by a person b) patients have more time than doctors do to wait (hours or days) for a response. It is quick and efficient for providers because they can answer calls when it suits them, evaluate the message and decide how to respond without your input. This divorces patients from initiating their own care when they feel they need to. It also means that if it causes or prolongs difficulty as a result, that's acceptable and secondary to the way offices must be run.

Suppose that the patient is elderly and too sick to wait hours for a response, unsure if they need an appointment, a prescription or a phone consultation. One patient told me, she needed to speak with someone about her situation which had changed rather suddenly. But when she called the office she got voice mail and didn't understand how to use it. After pushing the wrong number several times the recording told her she had made three inappropriate choices and her call would be disconnected. She didn't get through to the office and as a result went without the care she required. This meant a worsening of her condition and unnecessary suffering. The elderly have an especially hard time with these methods. The stress of this confusion and the uncertainty about the availability of treatment tells patients that providers don't care about them. It is a direct attack on the self-esteem of patients.

What has been created is a system that frustrates the natural drive patients have to return to a state of health. Consumers are trying to fit into a system that wants to deny input from them. This milieu is one that shows consumers their needs are secondary to a system which has become confusing and overwhelming to them. This has forced consumers into a defensive posture and redirected their energies away from healing to satisfying the needs of healthcare providers. Our healthcare is a system of exile. It is controlled not by the people who support its existence but those who take advantage of it in the form of corporations. Workers are in a task oriented mode that does not allow for individual needs and the dignity of those who rely on it for medical care. Experienced staff has given way to inexperienced people without adequate training to understand people and their needs. It is a system guaranteed to make recovery from illness more protracted than it should be. This is a system that has become part of the disease process itself.

The current trend of forcing patients into HMOs for their care has created an increase in the need for primary care physicians, most often family practice physicians. The function of the family practice doctor is to provide the initial evaluation of a problem, begin treatment and if necessary refer patients on to specialists. The objective is to keep patients out of the offices of specialists thereby keeping costs down for insurance companies. Insurance companies do not want patients evaluating their need to see a specialist. The basis for this is that patients are not qualified to determine what type of care they need and so will visit specialists unnecessarily. Unfortunately, the same can be said for many family practice doctors. It is the job of the family practitioner to treat patients from the pediatric to elderly patient. He must make the initial evaluation for the full gamut of disease and injury. In short, he must provide treatment for every area, and be able to discern what he is qualified to treat and which require more sophisticated therapy. Family doctors are expected to provide care for all conditions before referring them on, if treatment doesn't bring the desire result and the condition persists. In other words they are applying the same "first line" treatment that a specialist would. This assumes that a family doctor is applying the same level of diagnostic skill that a specialist would when initiating treatment. Not just the same expertise at triage and initiation of therapy but for all the various types of disease and injury. That requires a level of skill that surpasses even the specialist who treats a narrowly defined group of diseases.

How does a family practice physician know so much about so many different problems? How does a physician assistant or nurse practitioner (who often see patients in the physician's stead) keep up with all they need to know? Medicine is a field that is constantly changing, much of it is very rapid change. It is a field that is increasingly discriminating and refined. Often the proper diagnosis is dependent upon the subtleties of an increasingly sophisticated interpretation of tests and symptoms. Is it reasonable to presume that family practice doctors and their staff are always up to speed? Even specialists must make a concerted effort to be current on just their own area of expertise. This is a line of reasoning that refuses logic and yet insurance companies continue to force doctors to see patients they are not qualified to be treating and patients are not being allowed to see a more expert practitioner. Even if a referral is made by the primary doctor it doesn't mean the patient will allowed to see the recommended specialist. HMOs are so restrictive that the opinion of the family practice doctor alone is not enough to get a patient into see a specialist. Family practice physicians are in a unique position. Insurance companies want everyone treated in the family practice office ostensibly because these doctors are so good at diagnostics and treatment. But at the same time the insurance industry tries to second guess these doctors by having all referrals reviewed by doctors who may or may not know the patient being referred. It is therefore not up to the patient's personal physician to decide the referral but up to a review panel. This is a time consuming process and patients who cannot wait on the process may have to pay for the referral out of pocket.

Medical diagnostics are increasingly complex in both theory and technology. New equipment is more intricate which means it requires increased training to use it. New technology demands expertise to interpret the results of the tests done with new technologies. Minute alterations or subtleties that are easily overlooked can be extremely important in both diagnosis and treatment. Also the frequent use of these advanced methods is important to maintain a high level of skill for practitioners. Thus it can be difficult to stay current while carrying a full patient load. But more and more the correct diagnosis depends on details that may be inappreciable to a generalist.

The result is a trial and error approach based on the dictum that a certain group of symptoms will probably respond to a particular therapy. The diagnostic process then proceeds from general to increasingly specific. Sometimes this works but many times it does not and is lost while the disease continues to progress. Routine testing which has been in use for many years may also be subject to newer and more sophisticated interpretations. Occasionally you have a situation where a non-specialist gives too much treatment, killing a fly with a sledgehammer so to speak. In such cases a specialist can facilitate care with a more individualized plan. As family practice doctors and general practitioners are forced to see more patients and make less referrals the details and particulars of a patients condition can get lost. When details and subtleties are necessary to differentiate the various aspects of diagnosis or care, avoidable mistakes happen. Mistakes mean at the least a protracted recovery time and added expense. These are some of the factors that cause the transformation of care transformed into para-care. The expectation of insurance companies that these physicians be all things to all patients to reduce the cost of healthcare is absurd and can be disastrous for some patients. Common diseases may require uncommon perceptiveness to diagnosis and treat.

There is a place for primary care in the system. They have done and can do a great deal more good. They are somewhat better able to the coordinate treatments for several problems at one time. They also tend to be more accessible with shorter waiting times.

A primary care physician with experience and perception can overcome some of the obstacles put in his path by a corporate system. But to allow these physicians to do what they do best the system must re-evaluate their role in it and provide them with the support they need to do their jobs well.

There are problems with specialists just as there are with primary care physicians. Some are very expensive and it can be very difficult to get an appointment with them. Their area of focus is quite narrow and they think much less about coordinating care with other doctors who may be treating the same patient. In fact rather than treating patients as they have in the past they tend more to doing the diagnostic work and let the primary care physician actually treat the patient. This is at best a very haphazard way of doing things. Specialists consider themselves more expert and above other physicians in status. This can set up an awkward dynamic for patients when they sense competition between their doctors. This is most obvious in smaller communities. They become big fish in small ponds. These doctors become experts not as a result of their personal expertise but simply because they have chosen a specialty area of practice. The honor and integrity of physicians is to be found not in fact that they have acquired physician status but on an individual basis. Any set of circumstances can be improved by dedication and respect for patients. Each physician must decide for himself if he will resign himself to the system or work to improve it in the interest of his patients.

Another important aspect of office care is having procedures that were formerly done in the hospital moved into the office setting. Safety as always must be the most important consideration. But the patient's level of comfort during the procedure is also very important. When judging safety one must think about what may happen if an emergency situation arises during an office procedure. You should understand if sedation is required, who will do it and what it consists of. Not only must the physician be qualified to do the procedure but his assistants should have specific training in the type of sedation used. The level of sedation is important to consider. Will you be sedated but awake or actually asleep during the treatment. Cost is of course an issue, but office procedures are not always less expensive than those done in the hospital especially if there are unexpected problems. Some physicians are very good at performing a particular procedure but are woefully inadequate when things go wrong and emergency measures are necessary. Doctors like doing as much as they can in their offices because it saves them time and is very convenient. Those things should not be the patients concern however. The patient must do what he feels most comfortable doing. It can be helpful to ask your doctor very specific questions when choosing whether to have a procedure done in the office or hospital. The primary issue is how well a treatment suits the patient not the physician. You should find out:

What are the differences in the actual performance of the procedure between office and hospital?

When did doctors start doing this procedure in the office? How many has your doctor done?

What are the possible problems, and are office emergency measures adequate or would it mean transfer to the hospital if things go wrong?

What type of training do the assistants who will be helping your doctor have? Is your doctor (or assistant) certified to conduct the sedation needed for this procedure?

Does the recovery time differ from that of a hospital procedure?

Some patients will feel safer in the hospital environment and others will be more at ease in the office. It is a highly individual choice. Fewer patients are being allowed to make such choices however. But having a procedure done in the office does not make it less significant than one done in the hospital. Office treatment may in fact be fairly involved and uncomfortable for patients. Office procedures do not necessarily equate with easy procedures for the patient.

The hospital is the one place more than any other where the worst of healthcare is exemplified. The system's failures and the personal injustices of its individuals are acted out on it patients. The patient is essentially captive and so must watch all of healthcare's best and worst played out on themselves. It is the patient and only the patient who suffers or survives the "good and bad days" of their caregivers.

One of the most confused aspects of care today is where to go for care. Emergency departments have been turned into clinics, clinics have become urgent care centers and home health care often provides the same care a patient can receive in a hospital. As medicine becomes more sophisticated finding the right venue if you are a patient can be difficult and confusing.

The easiest process of admission for patients is pre-registration for elective procedures. But many come through the emergency dept. or are transferred from the urgent care center. These patients face the growing challenge of trying to get what they need in an environment that is alien to them. Busy emergency rooms are noisy with many people doing many different tasks simultaneously. The ER appears disorganized even though it is one of the most organized places in the hospital. The goal of emergency care is not the same as for other parts of the hospital. However, the philosophy behind it is the same. All of the attitudes patients encounter in healthcare are true here as well.

The usual expectation of patients is that the people in the ER function the way other hospital employees function. This can be disconcerting to patients who have been in the hospital but not the emergency department. The objective of emergency care is to revive and or stabilize seriously compromised patients. This may result in a slightly different protocol for procedures. These differences can be stressful for patients and their family members. The emergency room environment is a microcosm of care focused on trauma and constrained by time, urgent situations, and a high number of patients. Both families and patients may be thrown off guard by the complexities and pressures of the ER. But the priority for consumers must continue to be safety. In so far as possible people must try to get explanations of what is being done to and for them. Family members and patient advocates must do the same. The unfortunate similarity of emergency rooms with other areas of the hospital is that neglect and mistakes happen there too.

Whether coming in by the front door for a scheduled procedure or through the Emergency Department, once in the hospital the patient is exposed to a dizzying array of hospital personnel. It would be difficult to try and understand the function of everyone involved in direct patient care. However, the more you know the better prepared you will be when encountering the attitudes and ineptitude of some hospital workers. No one - not anyone - should be in the hospital without designating someone who will have complete access to information about your treatment. If at all possible the hospital and your doctor should be informed of who this is before your admission, or it should be done as soon as possible after admission. For people with chronic illnesses your doctor should know who this is even without hospital admission being an issue. Having a friend or family member has several advantages. The first is that it provides another set of eyes and ears watching out for your welfare. Mistakes may be made and it is easier to catch them early with two people acting as observers. Second, it serves to let hospital staff know that you are important and by extension your care is important to more than only you. Hospital personnel dislike having to answer to patients and even less to a patient advocate. But they must realize that only the best of care is expected for their loved one. Third, the hospital environment is so demanding for patients that the extra patient support provided by an advocate can spare the patient some lost energy that can then be directed into healing.

Whatever issues arise during a hospitalization it should be remembered problems are authored by a system created to support itself, and to do this it uses the consumer. For the patient this means working through problems at the level of floor nurses. This is where the priority is task completion, interruptions to the routine (by questions or problems from patients) reduce the number of tasks completed. What nurses have known and patients do not is that the job of floor nursing is a job that cannot ever be completed. It is a physical impossibility for nurses to have served patients as completely and carefully as they need to. The patient load is too heavy and the staff too small. Hospital nursing is a set-up for the failure of nurses to be able to do those things they know and want to do for their patients. The sadness nurses experience and not having the manpower they need to fulfill not only role for themselves but also patients is very demoralizing. The poor morale of hospital staff is a chronic, underrated problem that can seriously effect the welfare of patients. People who are unable to do their jobs well due to factors they can't control may give up trying to do a good job. When staff don't do a good job patients get hurt.

Hospitals routinely expect complete patient care to be done with incomplete staffing requirements. In recent years the level of staff required to keep patients safe has begun to lag behind common sense and reason. As the numbers of nurses decrease, the tasks of patient care each nurse must complete rises. Nursing care is composed of carefully orchestrated medical minutia. Nurses despair knowing that they are charged with doing more than one human being can possibly accomplish in an eight hour workday. This one fact does more to erode worker morale and patient confidence than any other aspect of hospitalization. This lack of support by the hospitals nurses are employed by alters attitudes as well actual care. This may be in the form of hostility, resigned disregard, or complacent understanding that the unattainable is the status quo. It is a terrible price to pay for both patient and nurse. This doesn't mean however that nurses are without the potential to do a great deal of good for patients. But it does mean that nurses must find their own personal way of coping with long hours and the frustration of their nursing ideals.

Of all the hospital employees nurses are in a most unique position. They are caught in the middle, and are charged with making order out of what would otherwise be chaos. Doctors orders are discharged from the nursing station. If mistakes happen the nurse must sort out the problems and restore the situation. If doctors are unhappy they complain to nurses, if the lab makes a mistake or overlooks orders they complain to the nurse. If radiology is too slow getting a study the nurse must "fix it". Nurses are pushed and pulled in many different directions simultaneously.

The hospital environment is a place full of many colliding emotions and motivations for both patients and workers. That patients and staff will clash over items big and small should be expected. The elimination of conflict between staff and consumers has been poorly addressed. Up until now finding methods of pacifying both patients and staff has usually meant forcing the views of staff on a submissive patient population. The vast majority of patients do keep quiet out a sense of self-preservation. They save the recriminations and anger about unfair treatment for support groups and fellow patients. There is no amount of money thrown at public relations departments that can diffuse the emotion generated by the ill treatment patients are subjected in hospitals. Just as with any business if one customer complains there are a hundred more who would like to complain but feel they can't. For every "problem" patient who dares to complain there are many more family members, friends, and patients out there comparing notes and making critical assessments. For decades nurses and staff have deluded themselves into thinking that complaining patients don't make valid judgments and that their complaints are isolated. A bigger mistake has never been made.

Problems encountered in hospitals by patients must be looked at as both systemic - system created and sustained - and personally individualized. Added to that is the completely unnatural environment of a hospital ward. The staff may be more familiar with their medical environs but it is no more natural to them than it is to patients. A hospital is like no other place on earth. Indeed, it is designed to be as unlike our normal atmosphere as possible. Everyday life is fluid, changing as need requires. Hospital are created to be impervious to change, relying instead on the their predictable responses to challenge. It is important to create uniformity in a medical setting, but it should not be used to negate the value of the individual patient's view of his experience. Reliability of technology to create a proper medical answer to physical problems is desirable. But it is not desirable to restrict patient response to the rigidity of healthcare workers. Particularly when controlling the patient's response means eliminating verbalized criticism of caregivers. The personal retaliation of staff toward patients is commonplace and patients are accustomed to weighing it against the advisability of complaining. The superiority of staff over patients is so solid in the minds of most hospital employees that even the most well founded complaint properly addressed engenders negative repercussions. We have already discussed how patients are maligned in the charting process, but the verbal abuse of patients is just as prevalent. When the abuse happens in a patient's room it is a simple case of patient against staff, one's word against another. This is another reason for the presence of a patient advocate (or even just a visitor) to be with patients as much as possible. It is always advisable to have a witness who will corroborate what the patient has experienced. When patients require help with moving about, bathing etc. The opportunity for physical abuse exists. Angry staff members can be unnecessarily rough toward fragile patients. Hospitals are pressurized situations where it can take only a small incident to trigger a damaging situation for patients.

Patients who try to bring attention to the mistakes and abuses of the American healthcare system should be looked upon as pioneers. It is difficult to draw attention to problems when patients are ill, it takes energy and courage. The response (if there is one) is usually negative. Patients who expect an improvement in unsafe or degraded situations can expect to be treated unfairly or isolated. Society has always abhorred the whistle-blower and healthcare cases are no different although they may be more individualized. It is an area where the poor treatment of patients has been virtually ignored to date. Hospitals have been given license by virtue of a silent public to treat consumers in any manner way choose. It is the public that must stand together and demand to be treated with dignity.

Healthcare consumers do have influence. It has gone long unrecognized but it is there to be made use of. Patients can and must redirect the minds of healthcare providers. There is no cost involved when fairness and human dignity are the goal. The petty concerns of status or ego can be eliminated if the public consumer chooses to the apply the pressure needed to effect change. Patients and families have permission to complain about being badly treated. They have it because they are human beings with worth and authority that cannot be removed by any circumstance or person.

When clinicians treat patients in the hospital (as in the office) little things badly done can have disastrous results. It would seem that a technician capable of understanding and using complicated equipment would not be careless in its operation. But human beings are imperfect. They can be forgetful or make a mistake not realizing it is mistake before harm is done. We have all heard the stories of respirators coming unplugged and patients who die from lack of oxygen and other similar mistakes. That is why it is always necessary for patients to watch what is being done for them. Patients must rely on their own common sense to monitor their care.

Everyone knows that nothing will flow through plugged or clamped tubes, and that tubes need to be checked periodically. If intravenous fluids are given, the principles of common cleanliness tell us that tubing should not be allowed to become contaminated by unsterile surfaces during set up or changing. It stands to reason that patient rooms be cleaned correctly and frequently to decrease the possibility of infection or cross contamination. These common everyday practices can lead to serious infection and needless traumas when not properly attended to. These "little things" can get out of control very quickly. The unspoken expectation of patients is that if hospitals can manage very complex kinds of care the "little stuff" takes care of itself. But this just isn't so.

These are the types of issues that patients have control over by bringing them to the notice of staff. Patients must always speak up when they observe problems. It won't win you any popularity contests but by being observant and acting according to common sense you can make the care you get somewhat safer. Good hospital employees won't mind having these reminders, but some will take it as an affront. When quality care is a priority for workers they will respond by correcting the situation without being difficult about it. If you get a poor response to your comments about your care, you can be sure your welfare is not uppermost in the mind of your caregiver. This type of immature attitude produces stress for all patients. It is another way of saying patients don't matter to personnel. No matter how someone responds to you, safety is the most important issue. Doing those things necessary to keep patients safe should never cause discomfort to caregivers.

It is imperative that you understand every aspect of your care. Whatever you don't understand, get someone to explain. If hospital personnel resist this (and they probably will) have your doctor go over what you don't understand. Employees who have problems with family and friends are those who expect to do as they wish, answering only to themselves. These are the people most likely to cause harm to their patients in the clinical situation. There are few (if any) families who are so difficult that they pose real problems for either staff or patients. But the mistreatment and exclusion of families from the treatment process can and should create problems. Hospital employees who are truly doing their jobs don't have problems with people who are present to give love and support to a patient. Whether systemic or individually based, the problems that providers have giving correct care are those that they themselves have created. Patients have sacrificed with their suffering to support a system that has chosen not to respond to the demands of dignity and fair, quality treatment. It also requires an examination of the attitudes and performance of healthcare workers.

In addition to the judgments one must make about hospital workers in order to protect oneself, it necessary to understand the extent of nosocomial infections and periontogenics. Nosocomial infections are those acquired while the patient is in the hospital. Periontogenics is a new term referring to damage done to patients by the mechanical equipment used in hospitals today. In his book Spiritual Healing in a Scientific Age, author Robert Peel quotes cardiac surgeon D.E. Harken:

> The complicated but life-saving science fiction world of Intensive Care Units has produced a series of diseases of and in itself. There have been psychological disadvantages including fear, insomnia, and the disturbance of diurnal and circadian rhythms. There have been mechanical disadvantages stemming from the improper use of respirators, endotracheal tubes and other equipment. There have been electrical hazards varying from simple arrhythmias to burns and electrocution while utilizing otherwise life-saving equipment. There have been chemical and bacteriological or infectious accidents due to inappropriate patient segregation or incomplete device precautions in the Intensive Care Units and Coronary Care Units. Finally, human factors have included errors in maintenance, use and interpretation and trauma.

As hospital care continues to advance the technology once reserved for Intensive Care are now finding their way out onto the wards. As floor nurses are trained in more sophisticated patient care the hazards associated with that care are now affecting more consumers. Some of these practices are ostensibly to save nurses time without lowering the standard of care. But from the patient's viewpoint it means one more thing that can go wrong. Technology is no better than the people using it.

The attitudes of nurses in Intensive Care Units toward patients is somewhat different than on the floor. These nurses sometimes show less compassion and are more demanding of patients and families. The environment they work in allows for even greater ego inflation than other parts of the hospital. These nurses often perceive themselves as more skilled than nurses in other parts of the hospital. The ICU nurse is trained to use monitoring equipment and function in different ways than the floor nurse. Their skill requirements are different, not better. The hardest job in the hospital for nurses to do successfully is still the staff nurse out on the floor. One cannot assume all nurses are alike. There are those who do try to be what they should be to patients. Some are just as compassionate as other nurses. But when they are not, the ICU can create a level of stress for patients unlike any other.

One of the most overwhelming aspects of hospital care is the assortment of different workers that the patient comes into contact with on a daily basis. They usually fall within five groups. Nursing staff, laboratory personnel, radiology doctors and technicians, physical and occupational therapy, and social services. These groups are really functioning independently and must answer to their own department head. This makes it almost impossible for patients if a problem of mistreatment arises. While a patient may complain to his nurse it is highly unlikely that the nurses will address a problem generate by a different department. The patient is usually on his own to find an effective way to lodge a complaint. Nurses should advocate for the proper treatment of patients regardless of who the patient comes in contact with. But this is no longer the case hospitals. Some hospitals have what they call a patient advocate. But this is a like putting the fox in charge of the hen house.

Hospital staff tends to be overworked with not enough time to really do their jobs as well as they would like. That makes hospitals dangerous. It really takes an extra family member to attend a hospital patient and see that they get what they need when they need it. This may mean the simple things such as fresh water or medications and treatments. Again, the role of a patient advocate of the patient's own choosing is imperative. Your advocate need not be there every moment. Other visitors can help with the little things as well. But for safety and efficiency patients do seem to need outside help.

A manifestation of stress inducing behavior directed at patients is most obvious in the hospital setting although certainly not exclusive to it. The increased pressure in hospitals for both patients and staff accentuates both good and bad behaviors. Probably the most obvious is what I like to call the lab coat kow-tow. It is the assumption of authority one receives simply by donning a lab coat. There is something magical about lab coats. One instantly appears more astute, influential and important. Patients are expected to acknowledge and submit to whatever these lab-coated people want.

Unfortunately, people who have a lab coat without the expertise and intelligence to justify its wearing create problems for patients. These white coated persons are unaccustomed to having their actions questioned, and can get very defensive very quickly. Once confronted with the idea that they don't live up to the lab coat ideal in the patient's estimation, they can become insulting and in some instances abusive. If something isn't done right it isn't done right, period. So never let yourself be intimidated by a lab coat. The lab coat kow-tow is definitely passé.

While the proper motivation for hospital workers should be your welfare, many times it is not. Like workers everywhere they face the same life problems. When they are happy in their work they show it and patients feel it. The opposite is also true. It should not be expected that these people will "rise above it all". People are people regardless of where they work, even when the stakes are as high as human life.

The advent of home health care has been very helpful to patients who might otherwise have to rely on continued hospital or skilled care facility. Many insurance companies as well as Medicare have provisions for home care. Home care is very sophisticated in the types of treatment that can be supplied. Respiratory care and the administration of medicine and fluids intravenously can be given as well as physical therapy. Some physicians don't order home care because they don't know enough about it. If patients believe it might be an option for them they should contact the medical social work department of their hospital. Before accepting home care however patients must be sure they understand what their financial obligation will be. This is especially important for the elderly who have limited resources. Home care is a business and is subject to the same irresponsible an unethical practices when greed is the motivation. Properly done home health care is a tremendous asset, improperly used it can damage consumers and leave them damaged monetarily.

Chapter 4

Mediocre Minds and Medicine

"Ultimately, jurors find for people they trust, and physicians surpass other defendants in public trust." Christian Science Monitor 6-17-96

The following is an excerpt from an article that appeared in the Christian Science Monitor written by Hiller B. Zobel from the Massachusetts Superior Court.

"Hearing the evidence of surgical mishap and putting himself in the jury's place, the judge thought this was what one might call an open and shut case.

The testimony - and the exhibits - showed beyond a shadow of a doubt that the defendant surgeon had somehow closed up the patient's abdomen leaving behind a ribbon retractor, a piece of steel, 13 inches long, one inch wide.

Thinking about the malpractice trials he had superintended, the judge realized that over and over a physician who seemed to have plainly erred nonetheless avoided (or from the plaintiff patient's view, escaped) legal responsibility for the apparent mistake.

Still, when patients sue physicians, out of every 100 cases, the doctors win 80. No one can really explain why, in a society which is supposedly litigation-crazed, doctors seem, as a defendant class to such kind treatment by the citizenry - at least those citizens who sit as jurors.

But given the usual legal rule that the patient has the burden of proving that the doctor failed to meet the standard of the average physician practicing the defendants, the defendant has a built in advantage.

Another feature of the landscape that may in part account for the prevalence of defendant's verdicts is the tough-minded approach of the malpractice industry. In the early stages of virtually every serious case, a group of specialists reviews that doctor-defendant's performance. If these experts opine adversely, the insurer will try to settle the case. If, however, they give a clean bill of health, the insurer will not offer any money, at any time. The case will have to go to trial. Such rigorous pre-selection tends to bring to court those cases patients are least likely to win.

Another doctor-favoring factor is the overall popularity of doctors, as compared with, say, judges, lawyers, or journalists. Some skeptics think that even where the evidence is strong, jurors affection for doctors simply causes them to disregard it.

As the judge mulled over the can't-lose cases in which he had seen patients fail, it seemed to the judge that the controlling cause was not the so-called jury-nullification, but a much homelier matter: In malpractice cases, as in all litigation, how the jurors relate to the individual parties is much more important than the strength of the evidence.

Whether the issue be a forgotten ribbon retractor or an overdose, happy is the litigant whom the facts favor; blessed is he whom the jurors esteem."

Because our culture prizes technology so highly, the person with the most technical expertise wins the approval, admiration and respect of society. This deference given because of their ability to manipulate what is to many an esoteric body of knowledge. In other words, the mystique arises not from personal human attributes, it comes from a sense of lack on the part of patients. Patients don't have what the physician has; a language apart from their ordinary understanding, the authority to make life and death decisions (about patients whom physicians may know very little) and a system that protects physicians whether they are right or wrong. Is it any wonder patients assume a position of subordination regarding their doctors?

Practitioners and patients play out this form of the have and have not scenario daily. The power to create such a demeaning and misguided system has been conferred on physicians by themselves, unfortunately with the blessing of patients. It is now time to withdraw that tacit approval. The most appropriate and easiest way to begin the process of change is for consumers to modify their thinking about themselves. The patients must acknowledge their individual personal worth as the final authority when considering treatment plans. The way to health and healing must go beyond facts and figures. The knowledge patients have of themselves comes from a level of understanding that is not bounded by materialistic thinking.

Conversely, when patients go to doctors it is to collect a set of facts grounded in science and formulated into a corresponding plan of care. These opposite viewpoints have to merge before the correct treatment plan is created.

As Judge Zobel discusses in his article the mystique surrounding doctors is all powerful, far more potent than just the man himself. In this position, doctors do not have to communicate with patients on an equitable basis. Patients themselves perpetuate this in several ways. The first is by allowing themselves to be considered the physician's inferior where health matters are concerned. The second is by supporting the physician's agenda for treatment even when it is contrary to what patients feel to be in their best interest. Finally, patients do not realize that they know more about themselves than physicians can ever know. The value disparity between patient and physician and its enviability is illustrated by how patients address doctors. This silly fad of addressing physicians as "Dr. Bob" using first names instead of the last is an interesting if screwball attempt at humility. It appears to mean that people performing the role of physician are just like their patients, ordinary, regular guys who want to be perceived as such. This misguided appellation probably began in the offices of pediatricians ostensibly to put children at their ease. I myself have never seen a pediatric patient fooled by it. Children know doctors are not like the other people in their lives. Wanting doctors to fix problems and make them feel better is what children expect from doctors. A physician who calls himself Dr. Smith and relates with tenderness and a soothing manner is what children deserve. Nor do children want a doctor for a pal. Children want what everyone wants, humane treatment not pretentious name games. If physicians really wanted to be on the same level as patients (big and small) they would drop the title not the last name. Another favorite phrase among doctors (so much so that it has begun to sound like a mantra) is "I will get off my pedestal when patients get off their knees." Again stressing the position of physicians as the correct one. Telling us that physicians don't have to improve the status of patient care until patients instigate change first. Also, it puts the blame for their God like mystique on the hapless patient. This declaration is a not so subtle abdication of responsibility to the feelings of patients.

Stephanie Cook puts it poignantly in her book Second Life as she recounts her struggle with both cancer and medicine:

> Without bothering to identify himself, he takes a chair next to the bed and sits there, contemplating me with his hands

folded, chin on bent wrists, eyes half closed. I am too astonished to ask who he is as he bends forward now, looking at me even more penetratingly, although it occurs to me that anybody who would walk into my room with such self-possession and so little concern or apology would have to be a doctor.

Dr. J. makes me an offer: he will take my case - transfer me to his hospital and make every effort to cure me - if and only if, I guarantee no interference ….and by that he means (to be perfectly clear) I am not to ask questions -any questions- of either him or his residents. I am not to meddle, demand explanations, or get tangled in the issue of accountability. I would promise to be a good patient, and if I didn't know what that was, he would take personal pains to inform me. He ran the show his way. He meant it. He was too busy. He would brook no compromise, and he has spent this time coming to see me - his Sunday night - to be certain I understand and agree to my half of the deal…or we can say goodbye now and I'm on my own. He likes this understood. In advance. He will do the saving and I will do the getting well.

My choice seems to be between the denial of the basic rights - the willful assassination of the ego - and death. I actually hesitate before caving in and giving myself over to the ministrations of Dr. J. and Quimby hospital.

Attitudes like those described above are untouched by the passage of time. Technology may change and society may evolve, but these behaviors and motivations are preserved as if in a vacuum. Willing change comes not from purveyors of "cure" but the subjects upon whom it is thrust. It is up to patients to submit to the standards protected by time or to break free from them at their own risk. Most doctors do not understand that their behavior is part of care. But how do you separate it from care? Facts are facts, but they are manipulated by the personality of the interpreter of those facts. Today, that manipulation is a privilege that belongs to the physician. Physicians have always assumed that patients will accept their point of view about treatment. However, the best understanding of how scientific fact will affect the lifestyle of the patient is done by the patient himself. Until that change is made in the minds of physicians, patients will continue to suffer from the implied superiority of their doctors. And doctors will continue to usurp the decision making processes that rightly belong to their patients. Arrogance has implications for patients that go beyond rude behavior and a practiced indifference to the feelings of patients. The arrogance quotient (AQ) of physicians actually erodes patient confidence in treatment and escalates all problems inherent in doctor patient relationships. Some physicians whose AQs are off the chart may actually be very good clinicians. Those physicians whose behavior is consistently deplorable put patients in the position of having to choose between technical expertise and treatment with dignity. Doctors do not have the right to impose this choice on their patients but they think they do. The principles of our healthcare system are so skewed that respect for the individual is not a given but a throw-away.

Patients and physicians use a different set of realities. Not only are the realities differing but opposing. Consumers bring into healthcare the a-priori knowledge of a state of being present with them from birth. What we know as time, space and ourselves is separate from what physicians tell us about ourselves. But it is only within the context of our own self knowledge that well-being and illness are experienced. For patients it is an expansive point of view because illness affects all of what we do and are. The thoughts, feelings and associations triggered by ill health are those things which are central to the understanding of our existence. Therefore, anything that reduces those thoughts and feelings minimizes the totality of ourselves.

What physicians bring to patients is a-posteriori knowledge gained not from the experience of being but the dissection of being by science. It is knowledge after the fact. The mind is not expanded but enclosed by boundaries that restrict thought to current physics. This exclusive reliance on scientific fact implies medical supremacy over the perceptions patients have of illness and health. That influence is unchallenged until something goes wrong and consumers are hurt by their physicians. Human beings function with a knowledge about life that has existed as long a man has. When people become patients they are asked to set aside what they know of themselves and adopt a new idea of what life is. Not only to accept a new definition of man but one that changes almost daily as science embraces its newest discoveries. This exchange of the inner man and his essence for the man dissected by science epitomizes Nietzche's phrase "groveling before sheer fact".

Conflict is set in motion when the facts of physics attempt to explain the trials and tribulations of chronic illness. Consumers come to doctors with an understanding of the entire scope of their problem, looking for solutions concordant to the problem as a whole. Until patients and their "body of knowledge" are integrated into the body of medicine doctors will produce inadequate answers to patient problems. Medical knowledge is only one part of the solution to disease or injury. But the power of it is such that when presented with it we are fooled into believing it is the only power. Patients work to find answers for the whole, the only motive being to restore the whole. Today the a-priori knowledge of what it means to be human and complete is reduced to an irrelevancy by science.

Patients relate to the environment around them on an intuitive level. People caught in the web of chronic illness must adapt to a way of living very different than that which nature intended. This adaptation happens on a daily basis. Varying energy levels, amount of discomfort and strength dictate how the very ill will interact with their physical environment. This is in addition to the usual demands of daily life. The responsibilities of modern life do not disappear when illness strikes, they multiply. Many people are not able plan ahead because their condition can change so rapidly that the life of the ill person remains in a constant state of flux. Moderns bemoan their rapid paced lives and the stress it produces as they race to keep up with their obligations. Patients must learn to do that with a body that cannot support such a lifestyle. Today doctors feel sorry for themselves. They complain about being overworked in their own hospitals and offices. They give little thought to the fact that have their health and a large support system with which to meet their challenges. Whose accomplishment is greater, the patient managing his life in the midst of painful trial or the physician who is the center of his comfortable universe? Physicians have the luxury of knowing they chose their role, patients do not.

Patients must reconstruct the form of their lives daily or for some even hourly. Because of this patients learn to make rapid mental assessments of what is happening to and around them. When physical energy is limited problems are met using intuitive processes. This may represent a change for people who have not made conscious use of intuition prior to the onset of long-term illness. However, intuition is always available and it requires only an awareness of its presence to use it.

Intuition is a way of processing information rapidly, often bypassing logical thinking. It comes from within and cannot be eliminated by, but may be influenced by the external environment.

Because it is an internal process it provides a frame of reference which is already individualized and therefore more attuned to each patient than impersonal medical theory. That is not to say other ways of processing information shouldn't be used. Certainly we live in a world where we must rely on scientific facts. Physicians must not only use scientific research but be very good at interpreting and implementing it to treat patients. But intuition provides an immediate assessment of how this knowledge will affect the life and lifestyle of patients that science cannot. It also furnishes rapid insight about the character and motivations of the healthcare workers they come in contact with. Another reason for highly developed intuition in patients is that providers usually withhold a great deal of information about treatments, medicines, research and other things patients would like to know. This may be due to not enough time, or possibly too little confidence on the doctor's part that his patients are able to understand what he might say. To protect themselves patients begin to rely more and more on their own intuitive sense. Their ability to discern the potential for good or harm in healthcare situations evolves naturally out of necessity.

Patients who have had a serious illness develop a very accurate sense of intuition. They are extremely adept at reading people. Almost everyone gets a feeling of unease in certain situations and we know from experience that it is wise to pay attention to these red flags. In very sick people this sixth sense is functioning in an accurate, conscious, continuous way. This high level of awareness is a gift born from the work of long-suffering. However, this is a quality that does not endear patients to doctors and nurses. To be in the presence of someone who is very intuitive can leave those around him with a feeling of being exposed or caught off guard. When caregivers feel uneasy around certain patients but don't quite understand why this is usually the reason. But for patients this is a valuable asset in the clinical setting. Patients may be able to "sense" when something is not quite as it should be although they may lack formal knowledge of procedures. When this happens it is always appropriate for the patient to ask more questions or engage their physician in a more in-depth discussion about what is happening. Any fear must be addressed and alleviated before undergoing procedures or embarking on a treatment plan. It may be that uneasiness arises not from treatment but the person giving treatment. This too must be considered. No one should be forced to submit to care by someone they do not trust. That a patient doesn't feel right about someone is good reason to ask for and get someone else. People don't leave their cars with mechanics they don't feel good about and they should not entrust their health to someone who undermines their confidence in treatment.

Physicians dismiss the value of inner feelings and their role in healthcare which is no surprise. People with differing orientations to the same problem each rely naturally on their own experience to solve problems. The physician uses science, the patient calls on his understanding of what should and should not influence his health. Intuitive thinking and scientific thought should be complementary. The best physicians are those who think creatively and allow for intuitive insight. Many times the "gut feeling" a physician has about a patient will influence care for the better. It may cause him to pay attention to something he might not have otherwise. Nurses also may come to know patients as more than just a chart and case history. Nurses who have a good sixth sense about their patients are better able in many instances to anticipate problems and needs. Many healthcare practitioners never learn to think creatively or intuitively, but for those who do their patients are the better for it. Unfortunately, medical schools not only don't teach these kinds of creativity but do their best to rid their students of it. Conformity to medical protocol requires the elimination of anything except rigid, scientifically based conclusions. But the ability to bring facts together and see them in a new way to formulate improved treatment is a function of creativity and should be encouraged in all those who work with patients. Conflict between creative, intuitive thinking often results in friction between patient and physician. Patients may know something is wrong with them or wrong with their treatment but be unable to convey it to their doctor in a way the doctor finds acceptable. When patients are unable to find the "right" medical vocabulary to voice their complaints physicians may not pursue complaints far enough to the patient's detriment. This is particularly true when the early stages of disease produce no clear cut clinical symptoms. It is important for patients to realize feeling sick or having poorly defined types of painful conditions is not the same as actually having symptoms in the mind of a clinician. Feeling a particular way becomes clinical only after they are confirmed by x-rays, blood work or other diagnostic studies. Some physicians (as a matter of course) do less for their patients to relieve patient discomfort because it is not verified clinically. Patients get caught in the unspecified area of having a real disease without "real" symptoms. This can prolong patient suffering or actually cut short the patient's life as one such patient related to me. In this case the patient who had a malignancy removed from the breast began to complain of shoulder pain on the same side of the chest. She visited her family doctor several times complaining about the aching of her shoulder. The physical exam he conducted of the shoulder did not reveal anything specific in his opinion. As time passed and the pain continued she was sent to a shoulder specialist. He told her it was sore muscles or perhaps a mild sprain. When the patient ultimately pursued the matter (with another physician) it was determined that the cancer had spread to the lung on the same side. It is safe to say that most physicians would not have made such a basic and disastrous mistake. But there are those who will not consider patient problems as treatable until they are independently legitimized by clinical data.

The decision not to provide proper education to healthcare employees is something that has been damaging to consumers. It also erodes the talent and morale of practitioners who want to do their jobs well and keep abreast of change. The lack of ongoing worker training to keep costs down has a psychological impact aside from the technical aspects of medical procedures. The general lackluster performance (that plagues all of society) comes from employees who don't have the ability or desire to think carefully about the implications of what they do.

I have heard it said that Albert Einstein remarked "great spirits have always encountered violent opposition from mediocre minds." Although they are often maligned and considered intellectually it is the patient who is today's great spirit. The ordeal of coping with the healthcare system gives those who survive it a greatness of spirit that goes unrecognized by health professionals. The mediocre thinking of some medical workers is the greatest obstacle to improving the day to day lives of patients. People who have overcome the odds in spite of overwhelming injury or illness win our admiration and our hearts. Everyone loves and respects the cancer survivor who has won his struggle or the paralyzed person who walks after being told it was impossible. Just as they have earned our hearts so should the many others who continue to work and struggle quietly each day as they contend with mediocre and inadequate personnel.

The seriously ill are very clever about what is required to face the serious problems they have. Chronically ill people cultivate (by necessity) a level of practical perception greater than the average person. Their response to problems is often more pertinent and immediate than the solutions caregivers can offer. Patients are a vast untapped resource of creative skills that are not utilized by the system. However, it doesn't matter how applicable a coping method is, providers frequently won't use it if is the patient's idea. Seriously ill patients are chronically underestimated for their inventive adaptability even when it may enhance the work of their caregiver. To not make use of patient created solutions to problems contributes to the unnecessary suffering of patients. It is a message to patients that their work and courageous persistent is unworthy of consideration by caregivers. This is one aspect of provider produced stress - PPS - that is undeniably harmful. It is insulting for patients to be told by physicians that the methods which they find to be beneficial are unacceptable simply because it wasn't their idea. This type of petty behavior is typical in the system. As a result, patients are discouraged from participating in their own care. Most patients with long term illness are capable of understanding how to modify their care in ways that will satisfy medical standards. This is due to long time familiarity with their condition and treatment. This type of power struggle between patient and practitioner is routine when disagreements arise. It results from caregivers who have limited power positions and feel the need to prove their own influence. They may also be embarrassed by those better ideas that patients come up with. Patients see through this ego nonsense instantly, and the practitioner then loses respect in the eyes of his patient. Every illness has two parts. The first is physical and the second but inseparable and equally important is how to cope with healthcare workers.

When I was very ill I had a central intravenous line which was fed into the upper chamber of my heart. Its purpose was to provide a direct route for fluids and medications into the blood stream by bypassing the more usual IV pathway of veins in the hands and arms. Because it goes directly to the heart there is increased risk of infection and embolism. Keeping this line open and freely running can be a complicated, and sometimes arduous task. To maintain my line I had a nurse provided by the hospital who came to my home. These types of catheters are notorious for becoming plugged and then not usable. But between the two of us my nurse and I found a routine that worked for me. When I became hospitalized my surgeon refused to use the method we used at home to keep the line open. His rationale was "this is the hospital and we do things the hospital's way." There was nothing about the way the home nurse maintained it that was contrary to hospital standards or that would preclude the use of her technique. The surgeon's objection had a two-fold purpose, to tell me that my ideas were not to be entertained (even when they were right) and to show that regardless of outcome his word was law. For me this meant many frustrating hours as hospital personnel struggled to do things his way, making a bad situation worse. It deprived me of the use of my central line because his method simply didn't work to keep it running. I was left with a useless piece of equipment which remained in place at great risk to me. This example of unrestrained ego is typical of the attitude physicians have toward patients. Behavior of this kind diminishes patients and compromises their healing potential by creating enormous stress. Physicians continue to perpetuate this harmful approach because they have complete freedom to do so.

If you aren't understood by your physician your health is being compromised. When you haven't been recognized in an authentic and valid way, the skills and attributes you have are overlooked and valuable healing assets are lost. When the physician's perception of his patient is different from the patient's perception of himself the risk of maltreatment is markedly increased. The ability to understand another person and their struggle depends upon our own spiritual maturity. Understanding is a developed quality of response to others that comes from within. It is the recognition of suffering in others that exposes the need for change. The activating force of change is the ability to put oneself in the place of another.

The philosopher Schopenhauer is quoted by Joseph Campbell in his book The Inner Reaches of Outer Space. Schopenhauer wonders, "how is it possible that suffering that is neither my own nor of my concern should immediately affect me as though it were my own, and move me with such force that it moves me to action?" He goes on to say "Examples appear everyday before our very eyes of instant responses of the kind, without reflection, one person to another, coming to his aid, even setting his own life in danger for someone he has seen for the first time, having nothing more in mind than that the other is in need and in peril of his life." Patients do not expect doctors to make decisions based on emotionality or random impulse. They do not expect treatment to wax or wane because of labile emotion from physicians. But what moves physicians to action on behalf of his patient should be informed by the ability to spontaneously put himself in his patient's place. Without that impetus care is a sterile calculation just as likely to be cruel in its execution as is it to be kind. What moves a human being to assist another to the extent that he is willing to invest years in learning how to do so effectively is something patients recognize and understand. Patients look for it and have a right to expect it. Doctors who become doctors to satisfy their personal yearnings for status and economic comfort without first having a powerful personal identification with the suffering of others are inadequate to meet the full challenge of patient care.

Physicians are still reducing their patients to stereotypes. Additionally, women are still thought of as emotionally inadequate to cope with illness as well as men. This prominent feature of medical practice while outdated still lives on. Trying to see too many patients at a time and caring for many patients with very similar problems encourages the practice. They stereotype patients according to their illness category. Women are most often the recipient of this demeaning way of looking at people. "Women's diseases" such as Lupus, arthritis, chronic fatigue syndrome are only a few of the many diseases associated primarily with women. Patients with these diseases are frequently described as neurotic, demanding, fragile and uncooperative. These physical conditions were and still are misunderstood by many physicians. The increasingly complex study of the immune system is beyond the scope of many general practice physicians. This disease category requires testing beyond what generalists are able to skillfully interpret. This can mean diagnosis may be made primarily in the most obvious or serious of cases. For many years this meant patients were told their symptoms were unfounded and referred to psychiatrists for treatment of both misdiagnosed illness and problems created by the attitudes of physicians toward their patients. This failure of physicians to take the complaints of their patients seriously created a standard of degrading care that persists today.

The healthcare system was created by men. It remains the same "good old boy network" it has always been. Women were first allowed to enter into the system to do the menial tasks that physicians considered themselves above doing. Nurses have been given permission to labor at higher levels of skill not because they are capable of doing so but because it eased the workload of physicians. They were also expected to serve as hand-maidens for patronizing physicians. For the last hundred years female nurses have risen above the level of physicians by their dignity of service to mankind. That men have allowed women the opportunity to prove their talent for medicine by becoming physicians is not a great accomplishment. The change came slowly and many lives were lost that could have been saved if women had come into the system earlier.

Looks make the patient. As most women with chronic health problems already know, if you are sick you should look sick when you go in for your appointment. If you don't appear ill your problem may not be taken seriously. This is a ridiculous situation but true and it happens every day. This happened to me at a time when I was seriously ill. The female gastroenterologist I saw told me, I couldn't really have the symptoms that I described because I "didn't look sick enough". Not only was I sick, I subsequently spent the next three months in a hospital. No doctor I know would tolerate that type of behavior directed at themselves if they needed treatment. As doctors are forced to cut back on diagnostic procedures by insurance companies this superficial treatment will not only continue but get much worse. Simplistic as it sounds doctors must learn at some point not to judge a book by its cover. Patients who find a way to make themselves look good in the face of serious illness can and many times are considered suspiciously by their physicians. Physicians should be proud of these patients rather than doubting their story. Instead a good appearance may reinforce the idea that no real problem exists. Patients know that they don't need a medical degree to understand physician behavior. The aura of the medical mystique that surrounds physicians is transparent. That patients don't call their doctors on their bad behavior doesn't mean patients don't experience it. Physician arrogance is a stage upon which physicians feel free to indulge their private bigotry - with full immunity.

The compassion component when found wanting in the personalities of physicians can and frequently do render them medical misfits in the world of healthcare. The tired excuse that doctors use to explain the apparent absence of compassion is that rather than lacking compassion they are simply not good at expressing it. Hidden compassion is not really compassion at all but menial medicinal delusion. The first interaction between patient and physician must be a human one. Without this antecedent to care treatment may not have value to patients even on its most pragmatic level. What moves physicians to offer compassion moves patients to accept it. Patients also accept compassion with the understanding that it enhances their recovery process. The lack of real understanding of patients in the healthcare setting is made manifest by the way care is given. Caring insight is not a part of clinical protocols even though it can be integrated as a vital force to generate better healing. For physicians, the technical aspects of care take precedence over the emotional response of patients. It is appropriate that only the most highly skilled people perform procedures and design treatment programs for patients. But even the most skillfully executed procedure is incomplete when done without considering the emotional consequences for patients. Caring about how a patient reacts to their situation brings patient and clinician together through mutual understanding. It is the avenue by which a person becomes free to fully participate in their own care. When patients feel they are understood they feel respected. Patients who feel respected feel valued. When patients feel valued healthcare becomes a practical partnership. This allows two people with different skills and resources but the same goals to forge a practical partnership. Treating people without caring for them as individuals is degrading. It shows patients that they aren't worthy of personal respect. These attitudes of "care without caring" are a form of provider produced stress that is rampant throughout the system. It shows us the conflict between the principles of patients versus the physicians purpose as he sees it. Medical principles often collide with respect for individual patients.

Difficulty and pain, physical or emotional, are not the after effects of disease but the disease itself. When physicians don't respond to suffering preferring instead to focus only on the physical aspects of care they leave part of the disease untreated. A kind word or understanding touch can acknowledge the worth of a patient. Physicians and their co-workers must learn that the only acceptable way to treat people is to give care according to the golden rule. If caregivers cannot mentally put themselves in the places of their patients they should not be caring for them. Insurance plans, procedures, and all parts of healthcare put efficiency and cost cutting before caring. Today we find physicians using this as an excuse to comply with ways of treating patients that they know may not be in their patient's best interest. But many physicians have given up fighting for what they know to be right because they too are demoralized by a massive system based on profit instead of good quality care. But if physicians are demoralized patients are even more distressed. An act of compassionate understanding becomes more needed and more urgent.

When people are in the office situation talking with a physician they focus their attention on how he responds to them. They don't pay enough attention to their own feelings about what the doctor says. When patients over focus on physicians in this way they subordinate their own thoughts. As a result, many people walk out of doctors offices wishing they had said more or asked better more in-depth questions. They feel dissatisfied about how they just spent their time and money. It is the privilege of the patient to keep the doctor focused on themselves in a way that includes how they feel about what the doctor advises. Most doctors talk at patients and avoid getting involved with the way patients feel about the advice they give them. It is important however, because "how" patients feel about what they are told will determine whether they accept treatment. Patients must give themselves permission to react to what they are hearing from their physician. To evaluate the quality of an interaction patients should ask themselves:

Did the conversation with your doctor and his staff leave you feeling uneasy about the way you were treated, or uncomfortable with the language that was used, or his attitude toward you?

Did the doctor or staff give you the impression that they were more interested in themselves and what they were doing than how it affected you?

Was your doctor or his staff thoughtless, rude or argumentative?

Did the staff knowingly cause you unnecessary inconvenience or delay?

Did what your doctor say make sense in a practical way or did it sound too complex and confusing, lacking in common sense?

If you answer yes to any of these questions your healing aptitude and energy was diminished as a result of the interaction you had with your doctor. Anything that causes you to direct your energy away from yourself in a worrisome or unsettling way is draining, leaving you with less available energy for healing. If your conversation makes you skeptical that things are not being done correctly, the outcome of future situations may be negatively influenced.

To people working in doctors offices and hospitals these matters are trivial and without merit, and unpleasantness is something to be expected and put up with by patients. But whatever causes a patient distress is no small matter. People who have a chronic illness and are exposed to careless practices and poor attitudes of practitioners over a long period of time experience these behaviors as a burden. Patients learn to anticipate unpleasant encounters and will try to avoid them whenever possible. To be on guard against what you perceive as rude, degrading or even unsafe practices by healthcare workers erode the will to participate in treatment. The amount of energy required to keep oneself from physical or emotional stress and at the same time work to heal is more than people should be expected to do. But this is precisely what the healthcare system demands.

As people begin to realize that impersonal and unpleasant treatment is the norm and not the exception, the level of fear rises and confidence in physicians and treatment decreases. Just as consumers are influenced by the actions of healthcare workers, practitioners are shaped by the industry they work for. Society has shaped healthcare in its own image and from it has come the healthcare culture field.

"Instinct is better than misguided reason, even as nature declares."

Mary Baker Eddy, Discoverer and Founder of Christian Science

The greatest influence a patient can have in their care derives from their ability to change the context within which care is given. The first step to change is redirecting the focus of the physician or nurse. Is he listening to what you have to say or is their attention drawn elsewhere? Everyone knows what it is to try to engage someone in conversation when their mind is somewhere else. If you aren't the center of attention you must make yourself the object of their attention. The second step is to change your own thought, recognizing that whatever happens in that room must be to your benefit. And it is you who decides whether it is beneficial or not. These things are important because human beings are easily distracted and preoccupied. While this should not happen in a doctors office it does, just as it does everywhere. These are not issues of technique or technology but they are no less important to the attainment of good care. How does one become the real focus of attention? It may be different for one person than another. The direct approach is best. Simply say, "you don't appear to be listening to me." Physicians are adults and there really is no reason to be timid or diffident about what you need and expect. However you do it, you must be assured that you have one hundred percent of your doctor's attention. Without it there is no reason to believe you will get the best care your doctor can offer. Your instincts will tell you accurately enough about the character of the interaction between you and your doctor. Patients must learn to trust their own judgment about the attitudes of physicians before they place trust in the care they give.

After the interaction is properly focused (it takes a minuscule amount of time) you can see to the particulars of the situation. If his attention starts to wander bring it back before going further. You are the expert on how your problem is affecting your life. Therefore your doctor visit should be a meeting of two experts. You are on an equal footing with your doctor and must respect yourself in that way. Without that mutual acknowledgment your doctor visit will be less productive than it could be.

Chapter 5

Learned Quackery

Spirituality has many definitions expressed through many religions and philosophies. Unfortunately when it comes to spirituality and medicine the attempted blending of them by patients usually ends in one of two ways. The first is complete separation whereby physicians become superior and aloof as they ignore their patients wishes to integrate some form of spirituality in their therapy. As consumers run into this physician created wall they withdraw their feelings about the management of their own care and with it their sense of control over it. The second result is a semi-reliance on both medical and psychological spirituality. Unfortunately, blending spirit and medical means in the end will be the predominate force, eventually squeezing out anything else. Either way, spirituality is expunged from patient care and consumer rights.

Alternative methods of care are frequently a mixture of metaphysics, fads, and theories which can generate large sums of money for those who proffer them. Health foods both regulated and not, strange gadgetry, exotic formulations of alternative medicine and slick promotions for traditional therapy confuse and obscure the issues. This does not mean spiritual healing does not exist or newer ways of doing things are not valid. It does mean that whichever method one chooses truth and safety must be its main ingredients.

There are three categories of thought concerning the new ways of looking at healing. They are a) non-traditional b) new-age c) spiritual. They differ from one another although they are commonly confused with each other.

Non-traditional or "alternative" methods frequently refer to the use of herbs and substances derived from nature. Also included in this group of therapies are acupuncture and similar treatments. Eastern folk medicines may be included in this category. New-age thought is an eclectic group of many different ways of looking at health and healing and it too is often called alternative. The mind-body-spirit phenomena is one that combines eastern and western metaphysics with medical physics. In this context, spirituality and medicine come together to form a new perspective that people find more appealing than medical treatment by itself. Even a few

71

physicians are beginning to take up the idea that spiritual thought is useful as this way of thinking increases in popularity. The terms soul, mind, higher truth, physical body, spiritual body are also ideas with multiple meanings. But if there is a single unifying principle of new-age thought it is that people are composed of a physical body, a spirit and a mind which can be manipulated to focus energy on healing. This school of thought states that man is composed of material and non-material substance simultaneously. All of these elements combine to form the body and mold man's perceptions of the world around him.

Spiritual healing is lumped together with new-age thought by many people although its basis is entirely different. This arises because of the spiritual emphasis found in new-age principles. In exact terms, spiritual healing is not part of the mind-body-spirit phenomena that is so popular today, it stands apart from both alternative and new-age approaches. It maintains that God and his Spirit are not bound within the physical parameters we associate with the physical sciences. As such, the healing potential for man is infinite just as God is infinite. Nor should faith healing be included as a form of spiritual healing. Contrary to faith healing spiritual healing does not accept the finality of physical reality. Simple faith healing gives up personal autonomy. Thus it is up to God to respond to a request for mercy, by the temporary suspension of natural law. Spiritual healing actually preserves control of healing in the individual confronting illness.

Whichever method one chooses, it is important to remember that even the physicists of the day are acknowledging that a true study of the universe must allow for differing realities. The privilege to choose the method that is right for ourselves must continue as an individual, inviolable right. The imposition of one human system of thought over another can be corrected when found to be harmful or wanting. But some medical facilities use the patina of religiosity to dictate the role of healthcare in a community. This makes protecting health related freedoms a much more complex and difficult task.

For many Americans the time honored system of traditional treatment remains the norm. And at the same time are experiencing a resurgence of interest in what people like to think of as new-age treatment. This is not new, America having begun its exploration of new ways of thinking about healing in the 1800s. The Unitarianism of Europe, later in New England, followed by the Transcendental movement in the middle of the nineteenth century encouraged new ways of thinking. One aspect of alternative methods that needs to be examined is not whether alternative medicine is helpful but rather, is it really alternative? The motivation for using alternative medicines is the same as for traditional medicine, the removal of suffering and the restoration of health. Both methods manipulate the physics of the human body to affect that change. Practitioners of both traditional and non-traditional medicine make claims as to what they can accomplish with their machinations with vary similar methods.

Medical science has been oversold, promoting itself as something more than it really is. Billions of advertising dollars are spent in this country, dedicated to convincing the American public that the system "cares" about them more than it does, takes better care of them than it actually does and that it is scrupulously fair and honest. Society has come to believe in an image of healthcare that is not consistent with its reality.

Alternative medicine has included itself in that type of self-promotion. The fact that many practices of alternative methods are not sanctioned by the medical profession is one of its attractions. The romance of "natural healing" conjures up images of purity, helpfulness without harm in a gentle setting; not a cold, sterile clinical environment. Alternative medicine is oversold by the image makers as well.

Interestingly, there is a middle ground where traditional and non-traditional meet. That is in the offices of western physicians who see some value in combining methods. By embracing techniques newly approved by medical science physicians lend respectability to non-traditional approaches. Acupuncture is rapidly gaining acceptance by western physicians although the actual practice of it lags behind its approval. Acupuncture remains the same but now has a new image of respectability conferred upon it and therefor new adherents.

Regardless of method, the decision to use one method over the other, safety is always the most important issue: Medical practitioners warn against using any method or medicine not sanctioned by the Federal Drug Administration. For them, alternative medicine is characterized in generalities, dangerous at worst or ineffectual at best. Alternative medicine proponents accuse allopathic medicine of causing disastrous side effects and of iniquity by promoting what it calls harmful products and incompetent practitioners. Unfortunately both are correct in part.

It is never wise to stop traditional treatment to take up alternative therapies without discussing them with your treating physician first. Nor is it advisable to undertake new traditional treatment without a full understanding of its implications. No course of treatment should be started until you are assured in your own mind of its safety and efficacy. To find the real essence of a treatment means looking beyond advertising. Quackery persists in both traditional and non-traditional methods. Both use materialism to form their idea of healing and both rely on the image makers to sell it for them. That the American public is exposed to both without standards to protect the consumer from harm is a failure of our healthcare system. The issue is not one of a lack of concern for safety or shortage of organizations created for the protection of consumers. The real problem, as evidenced by the increasing numbers of consumer watch groups is that the methods put in place by providers fail miserably. Many thousands of people are injured each year in this country by unscrupulous and incompetent practitioners from all fields.

Most of the confusion about spiritual healing arises from a misunderstanding of what it is rather than its efficacy. To understand spiritual healing one also must look at what it is not. It is not a method of pleading or beseeching God to give us a pardon from misery. Nor is it a "helpful" adjunct to allopathic treatment to be used when other methods are not working to our satisfaction. New-age thinking is often called spiritual when it is not. Techniques like visualization are one example. Patients may be instructed to see in their mind's eye healthy blood cells replacing the defective cells causing illness. This is not an exercise in spiritual means helping medical means. What it really does is create a greater dependence on medicine. It does this by reaffirming that the matter composing blood cells is the ultimate healer. This technique is matter confirming matter's superiority over all. If this what someone chooses to use as a healing tool that may very well be the appropriate plan of care.

But it is important to clarify what is really material and what is spiritual so that any choice is undertaken with a full understanding of what it is. Confusion of terms may also result in a misunderstanding of what results to expect. Confusion about the basis of treatment may also compromise patient safety.

The conflict between spiritual methods of healing and medical physicians originates in the way science views life and the cosmos. For people who believe all reality must be verified by the physical sciences there is nothing to said about spiritual healing. If only those ideas sanctioned by scientific observation are valid we must resign ourselves to looking at and experiencing the world in severely restricted ways. Limiting healing thought to that which laboratories can create and replicate exemplifies the ultimate in human egotism. That life must be confined within the circumference of natural physics as interpreted for us by scientists raises man to the level of deity and reduces God to the level of man. If life is to be governed by the circumstances of medical expertise are we then at the mercy of fateful chance? Or are we to plead our case to an anthropomorphic God who may issue a reprieve from natural law in order to save us? For those who recognize Life to be more, spiritual healing is a natural process as relevant today as it was two thousand years ago.

When physicians fail to produce the desired result whether by bad judgment or bad luck the practice of medicine becomes an art not a science. Mistakes become more acceptable when medicine is regarded as art because art is not expected to be exact. Therefore, the higher standards of science no longer apply. What is semantics for physicians can often mean heartache for patients and their families. The underlying foundation for this is that when things work right it is the result of science and when treatment fails it is an act of God. Not only does this undermine faith in medicine it undermines faith in God.

The ideals of health are more than abstract principles. They become concretized in the exchanges that pass between physicians and patients. An attitude that some things are beyond man and God is the root of hopelessness. If physicians hold that survival is left to medical circumstance what can medicine or faith really benefit? Everything that we believe about healthcare eventually makes its way to patients and effects the return to health. The dependence of our culture on science to tell us what is in our best interest has become the standard by which we judge all things. For personal issues we rely on psychology, for health we use medical doctors and for the future we look to the scientist to tell us how to proceed. We also depend on science and technology to make judgments for us about the quality and meaning of life. Perceptions of ourselves are shaped by reality as science perceives it. By relying on technology to the extent we have, the spiritual connection to health has been lost. We think first of medicine and last of spirit to advance the healing process.

It is the absence of a common understanding between system and consumer which leaves many people feeling excluded from the process of care. The inhumanity of healthcare is evidenced by feelings of helplessness on the part of patients. This is not to say providers intend to create inhumane care. And healthcare recipients are not taught the necessary skills with which to interpret technical care. Care created for the masses is not meant to be understood by the masses. But there is another standard we can use in a healthcare situations. It is simple and effective. Patients will not understand the intricacies of surgery anymore than every airline passenger knows how to fly the airplane. However, patients do understand the qualities the surgeon should possess (skill, integrity, attentiveness) and bring to the operating room. These attitudes and attributes have a direct effect on care and can be readily observed by the patient. Thus, even without technical expertise the average person can be involved in the improvement of his own healthcare.

Spiritual principles can be applied to situations we normally think of as being strictly medical. For health and healing the greatest asset a patient has is himself. One of the ways to realize your healing potential is by utilizing your spiritual perception. Physicians know your situation in a very limited way. Rather than being limited however, the power of our spiritual reality is boundless and always available. To know the physical limitations of the human body is to know only part of what it means to be human. For a physician, what he can understand with physical fact finding is what he has to work with. Patients have much more to work with. The objective of spiritual work is to bring God, Spirit, to bear on the situation by shifting perception to this spiritual reality. As the reality of Spirit is perceived in place of finite physical reality our material circumstances change. The use of spiritual principles in the healthcare setting must be practical and immediate to be effective. Spiritual perception requires that it be useful for everyone. God, Spirit, is omnipresent and so must be His qualities of perception, justice, and intelligence. To avail ourselves of these qualities we have only to recognize the presence of the Divine and its qualities. Unlimited in quantity and always good, this support is readily available, always with us regardless of the situation we may find ourselves in.

The implementation of these qualities for the purpose healing demands that we direct our thought to them and discern their influence. In the clinical setting, knowing how these qualities are expressed is key. The human expressions of intelligence, justice and perception are found in motive. By understanding the intentions of physicians and the people who work for them we can improve the quality of care. Motivation will influence how something is done. If the approach to a situation is wrong the result is compromised. With spiritual thinking we can facilitate the correct approach for working within a medical framework. For caregivers, motivation falls into three categories.

> Humanity based - caregivers who perceive patients as people not unlike themselves, who need undivided attention given fairly, guided by intelligent reasoning.

> System supported - caregivers for whom the highest priority is maintaining their place in the system. These are people more concerned with getting their paycheck than helping patients.

> Personal - people who derive self-importance and status from their position and for whom patient care is an exercise of power.

These attitudes modify the care that people give to others and influence care positively or negatively. Suppose you are in the hospital to have a medical procedure done, an endoscopy for example. This is a common procedure in which a tube attached to a camera is inserted through the mouth into the stomach. It is used to check the esophagus and stomach for problems and to take tissue samples for biopsy if needed. The patient is attached to a monitor and sedated by drugs given through an IV. He is monitored for oxygen level, possible bleeding and his vital signs are watched. After the procedure when he is fully awake he is sent home. For you and your physician your safety should be the first priority. The way doctors and nurses relate to you tells you something about how safe you are. While your nurse may have good skills it won't do you much good if her interests are divided. In this case, there are many things that need to be done prior to even the most uncomplicated procedure. The treatment room must be cleaned properly and restocked with supplies for the procedure and any emergencies that could arise. The medications that will be used must be checked for their package integrity and date. These are simple, common sense things. When I underwent a similar procedure, the nurse failed to restock the room I was taken to. The equipment needed to properly complete the treatment was missing and this resulted in an inadequate procedure. I therefore had to undergo a surgical procedure at greater risk to me in order to undo damage from a simple mistake that should not have happened.

When your caregiver is rude, defensive or distant his focus is not on you but somewhere else. They are reacting to you through whatever is troubling them. If they are feeling inadequate or unhappy in the work-place you will experience it. Their motivation for the way they treat you is personal to them and not in your best interest. This fosters the attitude of "just going through the motions". Clinicians are in a reactive as opposed to an active frame of mind. Rather than thinking ahead to possible problems and preventing them, they respond to a situation only after the fact. This creates a very labile situation that can be hazardous for patients. When your caregiver is motivated by the desire of one human being to help another you will know that and be benefited by it. Careful compassion is a quality of Spirit and is discernible by all patients.

You can perceive whether the motivation of your caregiver is supportive and appropriate to your clinical situation. Spiritual perception is the process of finding the presence of God, Good, in a situation. When the spiritual qualities of Good are being expressed the circumstances of a situation change to reflect those qualities. No matter how great the technical skill of a practitioner, the performance of those skills can be impaired by poor motivation. Conversely, the level of skill can be raised by the qualities of compassionate focus and an increased awareness of the patient and his needs.

The task for patients is to recognize and support the right intention. Or to redirect the inattention created by a wrong motive. If the stimulus of the moment for your caregiver is in your best interest you will know. The power of spiritual perception is such that you can discern motive and know if the situation is one where the outcome of good is being fostered. Patients will not know if procedures are done exactly right and won't understand everything the doctors and nurses do. Patient security is not just a task but a feeling. Distracted personnel jeopardize patient feelings of safety and patients may feel the potential for harm before practitioners realize it. Thus, heightened patient perception may warn you about potential problems which might become lethal negligence. When Spirit is brought to bear on the situation the attributes and talents of those charged with our care are brought to the fore. This changes the atmosphere from one of just medical circumstance to one guided by the presence of higher thought. Care must be directed by principle not individual personality traits which may be flawed. Spiritual strength can also sustain patients when they are advocating for their own safety during treatment. Patients who hold fast to what they believe to be right for themselves can be up against a wall of emotional disdain from health workers. The most common reaction of workers to these patients is an immediate attempt to intimidate the patient. Shocked that a patient will take a position and hold to it workers feel the need to always have the last word on the subject. The simplest issue can become a crisis of thought for workers. For example, the spouse of an elderly patient asked about the condition of his wife. The nurse who resented the presence of family around her patient responded that it was illegal to tell him anything about his wife. He was not to know what the doctor said, lab results or anything else related to his wife's condition. When the husband demanded to know what was happening to his spouse which was his right the nurse brought in her manager. When the manager tried her hand at threatening the husband by revoking the privilege of even seeing his wife. The husband then demanded a physician immediately to tell him what needed and had a right to know. To avoid embarrassment in front of a physician about a situation that had spiraled out of control the manager launched another different attack on the husband. She demanded to know why he said his wife was not getting the care she needed. Why, she insisted, did he protest against everything that had been done for his wife? This even though he had never complained about the level of care. At this point the husband said that either he be given the details of his wife's care or she would be removed to another hospital. Now the manager had a public relations problem on her hands, this facility already faltering under a very negative public image. Because the staff on this floor routinely "put families in their place" they were ill equipped when this man who didn't bow under their transparent mistreatment. Not having experience at treating families with dignity their response to the situation was wrong in every possible way. It is not illegal to inform a spouse about care. When they failed to intimidate him they changed the question into a tirade about inadequate care. One simple question, what is being done for my wife? For staff it was an invitation to war. Absurd? Absolutely but made so by workers not patients. But this is the type of mentality patients must continuously contend with. It is rudimentary, bullying and routine. Contention like this is an unethical, integral part of treatment. If the spirit of Good is brought to bear on the situation it will be the product of patient effort. What guides workers like these is the absence of spiritual good. Does medical treatment need a spiritual perspective? It does indeed.

When you can't choose who provides your care you still have some measure of control about who will be present and where it will be done. Elective procedures can be rescheduled or postponed until you can be assured the people involved are really serious about doing their jobs well. Ultimately, its your body and your money, you are the final judge and authority. Spiritual thought can guide you if you trust it and yourself. Many people who are just beginning their understanding of spiritual healing don't feel safe using something other than standard medical therapy. For them there is still something to be gained by the study of things spiritual. Increased perception and awareness will help to guide people in choosing medical treatment that is best for them at the time. Spiritual healing comes quickly for some and more slowly for others. Different people will encounter different challenges. Also the degree of success one has with spiritual healing is appreciated differently by patients and physicians. The survival of a patient with a physician's diagnosis of certain death is considered a successful result by the patient using spiritual means. But if the patient has lesser, lingering problems, his physicians will use them to assert that a spiritual healing did not occur. Clinicians will always find something to cavil at when patients assert themselves spiritually.

The idea of using spirituality to cause healing is the journey of perception to perfection. How we perceive what it means to be healthy and whole changes according to what we learn about ourselves. To learn what the substance of life is in terms other than the apparently physical is the starting point.

If one understands suffering to be caused by God's will or to be something he allows to exist, the dependency on technology for the restoration of health is likely. If one views knowledge and technology as something given to man by God to solve his problems the reliance on medical means is probably great. When one accepts that the physical are spiritual are one in combination, both material means and spiritual thought will be influential in the healing process. It is medicine however, that will predominate when the spiritual and material are used together. For those who believe life not to be physical but spiritual, a greater understanding of spirit will be the source of healing strength. Whichever way one chooses to view it, spiritual processes are an unfolding of what we believe about what life is. At the end of it all is the great mystery. We can say however that where eternal life resides is a Timeless Totality that is everything and everywhere. The ultimate perfection of life is beyond what we know of material life. Therefore, the insistence of man to explain and create a materialistic taxonomy for the Infinite Spirit is nonsensical. Just as human beings can only get a glimpse of the infinite, words are inadequate to convey it. The current scientific view is that God does not become God until science defines what God is. If science gives spiritual substance the corporeal OK it suddenly becomes a legitimate point of view. But once spirituality is materially defined it is no longer spirit.

Most open minded persons would agree that the path of spiritual discovery is an incremental process. It is the acknowledgment of a reality that supports hope even when material means fail. The activating principle of life is always present. It is not a stop gap measure but an asset to draw upon from the first appearance of a problem. The fact that illness is conjoined with the search for the one Mind makes suffering a sacred journey. It is a pilgrimage that should command respect from all people in the healthcare system. Can there be anything more important than understanding life.? That it happens within the context of illness does not diminish its importance. A spiritual response to illness cannot be relegated to an inferior position by healthcare workers albeit they will try. The limitless higher self is not obviated by medical approval or disapproval.

Suffering does not exist for a reason or occur because we have something to learn. Suffering has no purpose. It is not directed at us from a supreme being because we need it. No one needs to suffer. To the contrary, individual suffering is the greatest threat to the future of the world today. Personal suffering creates dictators and despots who seek solace in the subjugation of others. Uncontrolled mental agony turns neighbor against neighbor. The product of suffering is more suffering. It is the search for the elimination of suffering that elevates mankind. Humanity is in the debt of every person who endures a painful affliction. Medical misery is a sacrifice for all who must contend with it. If the suffering of others was ignored mankind would not recognize the need to move forward and transcend the flawed idea of necessary suffering. Those who suffer become spiritual contemplatives involuntarily. They contribute to the elevation of mankind even though they may be confined to a sickbed. While this is the most ignored aspect of illness it may be the most important part. The meditations and prayers for the improvement of humanity that come from those weakened by illness are precious because of their clear vision and efficacy. Although one may be unable to respond to others as a result of injury or illness their presence is no less valuable to us. Spent in sacrifice these lives teach us all about the priority of compassionate learning. Prayer is contemplation of things higher than matter. Angels are a mental reminder that God passes His ideas to man continuously. Ideas from the mind of God cannot help but provide sustenance and protection in each and every circumstance.

Suffering regardless of the form it takes is not something to be accepted on any level. The suffering ones should not be blamed for the misfortunes of a disease they didn't cause and don't understand. Nor should they bear any guilt for its perpetuation. The cruelest thing one person can say to another is that whatever happens to us happens for a reason. In other words events are brought to us to teach us something. This is simply untrue. There are accidents in the realm of the physical universe. Some people cause the suffering of others for inexcusable reasons. But to say that suffering is something to be endured because it is meant to teach us something we did not know is rudimentary at best and harmful at worst. This concept is also at the root of hopelessness and perpetuates despair. Amateur metaphysicians abound in society today, and they can be every bit as dangerous as the careless allopathic physician.

The suffering sense is both personal and impersonal. It is impersonal because we accept a world where catastrophe and accidents are considered normal. What is accepted in the world regenerates and perpetuates itself in the world. It is personal only in how individuals reflect these concepts. One person will have a car accident and another may contract a disease. But we all express the underlying principles of the common beliefs of existence. We must therefore, assume responsibility for the woes of people we do not even know. If blame is to be attached to illness we all must bear the burden equally. We are all responsible for ending disease. Our role is to move from flawed human perception to the clarification of spiritual perfection. The illnesses of others is the sacrifice that shows the rest of the world which way to go.

Why is spirituality important to the practice of medicine? Because it intersects with patients who are on an important quest. What could be more imperative than the restoration of health? The journey is born from the essence of life. Surely it is as important as the role of physician. Does healthcare as practiced today have reverence for the real role of the patient? Not only does the system not express respect for patients it works in a systematic way to exclude spirituality from care. Physicians may be involuntary participants in this exclusionary medical mission but they must respect Spirit and honor it for the sake of their patients. The direct role of the physician in patient spirituality is a passive one. Theirs is the role of finite thinking, juxtaposed to the infinite resources of the patient who functions from an infinite spiritual basis. Healthcare workers must maintain a stance of unwavering support for their patients. The process of illness and the effort to overcome it should not be interfered with by the cold indifference of clinicians and bureaucrats. Neither should the immaturity and insulting behaviors of practitioners be allowed in the presence of one who has so much to accomplish as the patient. The numerous hindrances of small minded individuals is something to be avoided in the atmosphere surrounding patients with a long journey ahead. It cannot be stressed too much that healthcare providers must get out of the way of patients who are engaged in the healing process.

Medicine is as foreign to the body as is disease. The patient is caught between the two. To avoid swinging back and forth like a pendulum there must be something stable for patients to cling to. Transcending this wild ride is a necessity. How patients do this is up to them. There are as many ways to express illness and the fight against it as there are people. Clinicians are however, a very judgmental group. Tolerance of individuality is not something the system is prepared to accept. This situation has been sorely exacerbated by managed care systems. It has also given a silent stamp of approval to the obliteration of treatment based on individual need.

Patients are not enigmatic but they appear so to healthcare workers at times. Dissatisfied patients more so than others who are quietly compliant. Almost invariably workers attach blame to the behavior of patients. They call patients abusive when in fact they are not. But such a label gives workers permission to display their lack of understanding about what patient care actually entails. The proper response of clinicians to an angry patient is first to stand back and admire at their courage and strength. That patients are not completely beat down by the system is a marvel in itself. The second response should be one of self examination. Knowing that the care they give patients is pivotal to their patients anger.

How should patients react to mistakes and disrespect from caregivers? Overlook it? Forgive and forget? Neither option is appropriate. Suffering in silence is an enabling posture that promotes mistreatment. Submission to blundering conduct causes internalized stress for patients who are already under great stress. Worse than that it may lead to a deceased patient. I underwent a procedure whereby the liver and surrounding organs and ducts leading from them were visualized. To help picture them saline (salt water) was injected through a tube to expand the ducts and make them easier to see. This was done while the physician was looking at a picture of interior of my abdomen created during an ultrasound. The procedure had to be repeated some time later, done by the same physician. This time however was different in an important way. Instead of using saline to help him see what he wanted to filled his syringe with IVP dye, something that is commonly done. I noticed that he put something other than saline in the syringe and asked him what it was. IVP dye he replied. I informed him that I was allergic to it and didn't want it used. For people who have an allergy to it this drug may be fatal as it triggers a process called anaphylactic shock. This can cause the body systems to shut down in a matter of minutes. The doctor of course, took great umbrage at my statement. He responded with disgust that he had used the dye last time. No I said, and again asserted my objection to the dye. This time with undisguised contempt for me, he insisted it had been used last time with no problem. I countered by asking him to look at my chart. He stood up and went stomping off to find my chart. He returned red faced to admit I was right and no dye was had been used.

This physician attempted a procedure without having looked at his patient's chart, indeed he did not even know where the chart was. Had he been in possession of the chart he would have seen the allergy listed on the front of my chart. His attempt to make me feel bad about taking care of myself was a misuse of physician power. This in addition to simply being wrong about what he tried to do medically. Three mistakes that could have cost me my life had I kept quiet and succumbed, literally, to his belligerence. If and when a patient says no to something the discussion is ended. There is nothing ambiguous about the word no. No matter how powerful a physician thinks he may be he is no match for that one little word. It does not matter if the patient's decision is contrary to what the physician wants. Physicians no longer have the right to walk over the individual rights of patients.

Should physicians be forgiven for their failures? Forgiveness is not something one person can bestow on another. It is a state of being. Forgiveness can only happen when justice replaces wrongdoing. So long as the behaviors that cause harm exist forgiveness cannot exist. Forgiveness can exist only in place of destructive action not in spite of it. So long as healthcare perpetuates and approves its current methods forgiveness has no home in our system. The divine injunction is to love our enemies even though they may cause us misery and unhappiness. Love is ours to give. The patient's role is not to judge and forgive practitioners. To love one's enemies is to see their true being apart from the wrong we see them do. The higher self is the true self. It is that which is to be recognized and supported so that it may make good manifest in human life. This particular physician has good in him and this good never intended to harm me. But safety dictates that we must guard ourselves against the actions that are not formed by Love. Time and justice will right the scales and mete out forgiveness in the right way at the right time. In this way wrong is turned to right and humanity advances. Our job is to see love and offer it even in the most difficult of circumstances after our safety has been assured.

Chapter 6

Iatrogenesis - The Disease of Silence

Iatrogenic - (of a medical disorder) caused by the diagnosis, manner, or treatment of a physician. Webster's Unabridged Dictionary

Incompetence is rampant in our society, from presidents on down. It is everywhere. In fact, it is so bad that the only adjective I've ever been able to come up with in the lexicon that adequately describes it is "staggering".

Vincent Bugliosi - from his book Outrage

- Of more than 600,000 practicing physicians 60,000-90,000 are practicing impaired from the abuse of drugs and alcohol.
- 100,000 people lose their lives in hospital each year due to mistakes made by their doctors and staff.
- 30,000 die from improperly prescribed drugs
- 24,000 die from mistakes committed during unnecessary surgery.

In the above cases of malpractice only 2013 actions were brought against physicians by the states within which these doctors practice. A small fraction of these cases resulted in appropriate censure of physicians. Only one percent of healthcare dollars spent in this country is spent on malpractice insurance premiums. Patients who receive a judgment get only about 60% of what their injury actually costs them. If all cases undertaken by injured patients were decided in their favor and they received full compensation, insurance companies would still have a profit of hundreds of millions of dollars.

Denial and tolerance are the hallmarks of iatrogenic treatment in this country. Physicians support the system wide denial of bad treatment by making it economically impossible for their victims to seek legal redress. Physicians both competent and incompetent have no difficulty coming together to influence the legal system and legislatures to enhance their practices. And yet they say they are helpless to prevent other problems created by corporations and insurance companies that are causing harm to their patients. The same applies to legislatures state and national who pretend to be helpless when confronted by the damage done to innocent citizens by the healthcare system. Physicians and the people who work for them labor to protect themselves rather than protect consumers. Physicians have spun a cloak of rationales so complete and fine that it is like the spider web that only be seen through the brightest sunlight.

To say that lawsuits brought by patients are profuse and frivolous is the rankest naiveté. Practitioners and legislators must feel if they repeat this untruth often enough the public will believe it. Congress believes the consumer is out of touch with reality so much so that tort reform favoring physicians and insurance companies is not only right but necessary.

Patients have experienced enough suffering to know that they are in the midst of a widespread, unchecked epidemic. This environment of system supported malpractice is lethal public health policy. It is state sanctioned destruction of patients and their families. Malpractice also costs whole communities money by destroying its productive members.

The backbone of iatrogenesis is arrogance. It is confidence on the part of physicians that a) the wrong they do will not cause them (physician) difficulty, b) patients either won't recognize the mistake as incompetence or neglect c) other physicians will support them regardless of their actions, d) most physicians have more financial resources to fight any action brought against them than do patients e) even if doctors are sanctioned the penalties for malpractice and negligence are so light as to be inconsequential. There is no legal incentive for physicians to come together as a group to work for the prevention of damage done to consumers by physicians and their agents. The moral imperative to stop iatrogenesis exists in the hearts and minds of patients not doctors.

The insurance industry has proven by its own statistics that defensive medicine and the threat of lawsuits are not increasing the costs of healthcare. Tort reform to stop the runaway costs of medical care is little more than a poorly thought out con job. This "reform" is not reform at all. It is new packaging to ensure that physicians, corporations, and insurance companies can continue protecting their wallets. The consumer continues to be damaged (or dead) and his constitutional rights abridged. The weak serving the strong, at the expense of the weak.

If the basis for malpractice is arrogance the fuel for arrogance is denial. In America policy both public and private, is to deny culpability no matter what. Healthcare practitioners are characterized by a reactivity out of all proportion to the merest hint of error. Some of this is due the fact that many workers are ignorant to the reality of how they are to legal challenges. They are too obtuse to realize that the odds of their mistakes coming back to haunt them are virtually nonexistent. No institutions are better at hiding mistakes and their resultant injuries than are hospitals. Negligence or bad treatment is instantly buried, usually within the first few minutes of an incident. Nothing will appear in the record of course, but more than that physicians will immediately begin the process of explaining away the damage done to the patient. Injury will be ascribed to a different set of causal factors. Mistakes made in the operating room or recovery room are covered up before the patient has a chance to wake up. Incidents that happen on the ward evaporate just as rapidly. A hospital employee has the backing of the entire hospital when he makes a serious mistake. Hospitals have a safety net far greater in scope than do patients. Additionally, the employee commits his damaging action when he is better equipped to handle it than his already compromised victim. Other workers are just as rapidly reactive precisely because they know they are untouchable. This aura of invincibility brings out the worst in someone with marginal intellectual and moral acuity.

Physicians have at their disposal an entire system ready (and eager) to stand with them regardless of what they do. They have an entire lexicon and materiel with which to intimidate patients into second guessing themselves about what has actually happened to them. Physicians lie to patients, other physicians, and anyone else who gets in the way of a smooth running cover-up. They also lie to themselves which is ultimately the worst offense because it perpetuates the mistreatment of vulnerable consumers. Medical schools stop short of teaching physicians how to handle mistakes. The adage for physicians to "first do no harm" has some come to mean physicians "cannot do harm". Physicians cause avoidable hurt to patients on a consistent, daily basis. Nor do they acknowledge or rectify these hurts with any type of constancy. While physicians should use their sympathy to direct their healing efforts toward the elimination of negligence, they expend their sympathies on their fellow physicians. Preferring instead to protect their comrade even in the face of blatant mistreatment of patients. They do this because "there but for the grace of God go I". Far better to reason that they too might fall victim to the ineptitude and carelessness of a fellow practitioner. At this moment in time the moral refinement required of physicians to take an active role in the protection and justice of patients is beyond many of them.

This leaves consumers in the curious position of deciding what must be their highest priority. Should it be availing themselves of care, or insuring their safety knowing that if something goes wrong they will probably be left alone to deal with even more problems? Safety in offices and hospitals is not the same for doctors as it is for patients. When patients think about safety they think of their own well being. Physicians think about their own well being too. Self-protection takes on opposing forms determined by whether you are patient or physician. Patients must become preoccupied with their safety.

Author Robert Peel brings forward the issue of the overwhelming trust patients have of medical care.

> The medical triumphs of this century are generally regarded as among the wonders of our age. Less well known is the extensive, documented literature challenging modern medicine's right to be accounted an exact science or even a socially satisfactory system of healthcare. This dissatisfaction is by no means confined to such crusading critics Ivan Ilich and Robert S. Mendelsohn, with their insistence that medical science still causes as many diseases as it cures. The criticisms extend through hundreds of sober medical reports, sociological studies, ethical disquisitions, economic analyses, legal decisions, popular magazine articles, and academic investigations.

As president Derek Bok of Harvard ruefully suggested He continues, "many studies have revealed that doctors make a disturbing number of major diagnostic errors", he sites a recent survey "of 100 autopsies at a prominent teaching hospital which disclosed such mistakes in twenty-two percent of the cases." As if this were not bad enough he finishes his report by saying, "The information physicians receive, the symptoms they observe, the outcomes of the treatments they prescribe, can all be affected by the ways in which they act and interact with patients. The decisions they make are limited not only by gaps in biological knowledge but by bureaucratic rules and economic pressures. In short, the doctor's world cannot be restricted to science or neatly divided between the known and the unknown. Considerations of many kinds are often jumbled together to form a picture of uncertainties, requiring the most delicate kinds of judgments and intuitions." The operative fundamental that medicine is sold as a science and practiced as an art puts practice and principle into opposition. Do practitioners pick and choose which set of principles to follow arbitrarily? It is the contradiction of art and science that initiates and sustains the high level of uncertainty in the daily practice of medicine.

The atmosphere surrounding treatment is fertile ground for the exercise of power by physicians. In truth, physicians do not have an automatic superiority over patients regarding treatment. There is no higher authority conferred with the permission to practice medicine. But this authority is mistakenly generated by consumers. A medical license gives a physician the right to make medical judgments, perform certain procedures and prescribe medicines. There is nothing that gives physicians the right to "force" the physician's viewpoint about what is best treatment on consumers. The manipulation of patients to accept a particular treatment, stop treatment, or influence the patient's family in a certain direction is not authorized. They have no right to be rude, arrogant or disparaging of patients in any way. The freedom to behave and make decisions for patients with secrecy - confidentiality - opens the door for abuses of power. Consumers have given encouragement to physicians by their silence to maintain the status quo.

Once when I was in the hospital the surgeon determined I must have surgery, which he himself would to perform. I had an intense dislike and distrust of this man but he was on call for my own doctor, so there he was. I refused to allow him to do surgery because I was not convinced of its necessity. This decision made this ordinarily disagreeable doctor incensed. So, he devised a plan to force me into the operating room. He told my family that without the surgery I would die. But, he intended to prevent that by withholding pain medication "until I begged to have the surgery". Unfortunately, as many doctors do, he didn't think through his plan too well. My family simply walked into the room to tell me what he said. At that point his planned cruelty turned my family against him as well as me. My own physician returned two days later. I asked him if in his opinion I really had to have the surgery. His reply, "of course not, what gave you that idea?" The plan to force me into treatment I did not want came about because of an ego run amok. The scheme to force me into surgery failed for the same reason. This is a doctor who has spent many years bullying not just patients but staff as well. Because he has been allowed to behave this way for so many years he was sure his plan was the right thing to do and that it would work. He was completely unprepared for the idea that it might not be well received by patients. He also believed he was authorized to take the position he did. That is the greatest threat of all.

The lack of response of states to monitor and take action against doctors keeps patients in jeopardy. Thus, physicians find themselves in a self-policing situation. That is to say there is no immediate, practical, productive oversight to protect unaware patients. The abuse of patient confidentiality allows this phenomenon to happen in virtual invisibility. The only people who find it difficult to obtain access to medical records are patients and their agents. Whatever information that exists about a patient is easily accessible to everyone but the patient, the one who needs it the most. Secrecy also poses a problem for other physicians when doctor caused negligence or malpractice causes more problems for the patient. The new problem must be explained away but the treatment for it as well. If the resultant problems are similar to the problems the patient had before, the doctor's job is easier. The physician "adjusts" his diagnosis to better match the current treatment. He may tell other physicians about the true origin of the problems if other physicians must become involved and continue to delete them from written records. The tricky part is that physicians must show the correlation between disease and treatment in the chart. They cannot record one problem and then order treatment for another. That would be absurd should those documents find their way to a court room or review board. So, how do you cause a problem, cover it up in the records, and then treat it all the while documenting treatment for malpractice which is itself excluded from the record? You do it carefully, thoughtfully and with the protection of your peers. These actions create long term confusion and cause inappropriate subsequent treatment. Unfortunately, it is done all the time. This is another reason for hospitals not letting patients get too familiar with their own medical records.

Can patients expect to protect themselves against malpractice? One can check with consumer groups who are trying to monitor healthcare quality, find out what the physicians credentials are, and if he has had actions filed against him for negligence or malpractice. The same can be done to learn about hospitals and insurance companies groups. This is vital information and agencies who collect such data (public and private) need more support in their attempt to better inform consumers about the dangers of treatments and practitioners. But there are two problems with this approach. There is not yet enough pressure on physicians to report and take action against malpractice. Instances of bad medicine are under reported and under prosecuted. This cloak of secrecy leaves patients at risk to injured again and again by the same institution or practitioner. The other problem is that many people do not have access to this type of information or do not know that such information exists. The elderly find accessing this type of thing very difficult, the illiterate or those for whom English is a second language are at a disadvantage as well. But even the well informed, educated consumer may be restricted to certain physician groups by insurance companies, and in emergency situations there may be no choice at all.

It is important to remember also that like other professions healthcare is practiced differently in one section of the country to another. The treatment for like conditions varies in different areas due to the "clustering" of physicians who practice with similar attitudes and styles. It is also necessary when possible to consider the performance other partners in the medical group. If you have problems with one you will probably have problems with the others. The converse is also true as the pleasing attributes will likely be shared (at least to a degree) by others in the group. It should not be overlooked that just as there are the technical aspects of medicine, a group of doctors share the same attitudes toward patients. Whether it is animosity or appreciation, attitudes grow toward patients as more physicians become involved in the same situation. This also means that the inadequacies of doctors in a group are more obscured. Doctors do not like to stand out from the group. Clustering can also discourage doctors in the group from trying new ways of doing things. Something new may not be positively received even if worthy of trying. For many physicians whose priority is not making waves, the old way is the best way of protecting oneself. To act as an individual in the group is not necessarily well received by the others in the group.

It is lawmakers who must make the change from a system that approves malpractice by its own ineffectual stance to one that will take action. Healthcare reform without malpractice reform is a license to continue maiming and killing citizens. Such reform is possible but it requires the active participation of the public. Consumers must take back the authority they have given to the medical profession. Physicians and hospitals must be made to answer to the public, not only a partisan congress. Patients must come together with a voice of authority that they know to be right. As always, it is the oppressed who must work the hardest and do the most good.

Each patient must learn to think in terms of how appropriate their treatment is for them individually and if it is safe. Remember, it must pass the common sense test. A few tips:

Don't agree to treatment until you understand it. Get it explained as many times as you need to, but be clear in your own mind about what you are getting into.

If medicines are prescribed ask your pharmacist about type and dosage. Is it the right the drug for your problem, is the dosage right, this is especially true if you are getting a prescription for a child. If you are at all unsure check and double check. Call your physician to double check if necessary. Physicians do make dosage mistakes and the death of children due to simple over dosage is preventable.

If you have the luxury of time and resources read about your suggested treatment modality. There are standard protocols (treatment plans) for each disease that are to be followed. If your treatment differs from the standard you should know it and know why. It may be perfectly appropriate but you should understand why that is. Many public libraries have medical information as do community colleges and universities. Theoretically your physician should provide you with all you need to know, but if you need more or question the information you have been given check it out with another source. It is a rare patient (or patient advocate) who is not capable of understanding complex medical information when it is presented clearly. It needs to adequately explained, but that takes time and so many physicians don't properly educate their patients. Some physicians are also irritated and or intimidated by patients who have a good understanding of what is happening to them. But better an unhappy doctor than an uniformed patient. Safety is always enhanced by good information. If you anticipate a hospital stay call the floor of the hospital where you expect to be and talk to the nurses about who they believe are the best physicians. Nurses are busy but if you can visit the floor ahead of time you can ask which doctors have patients with the fewest complications, which are best at pain management and other particulars that might pertain to your situation. It is only their opinion of course, but a brief, discrete inquiry may yield good information.

The new paradigm must be driven not by profit but patient authorship. Consumer authority is the only mode by which medical care and humanity can merge to create a viable system of care. What constitutes this authority? It is the full recognition and confidence of self. That right of self that was conferred upon us at the moment of our appearance in the world as an individual being. There is no authority of system or organization that can hold itself higher than the patient as he reflects the human spirit. Patients who stand up for themselves against inhumane and corrupt treatment are rarely admired for what they do by the system. Patients who are passive are accepted by workers and are not seen as a threat. Retaliation directed at patients from doctors and nurses in response to patient complaints is predictable. Patients who exercise their right to complain are routinely vilified by healthcare workers. Not only are their reputations disparaged but they put themselves at risk for even more physical and mental abuse by doctors and nurses.

The emotional abuse of patients by both hospital and clinic staff has always existed but the current climate of care makes it even more possible. There are two ways to conduct every medical procedure; the way that makes patients most comfortable and the way that makes them most uncomfortable. It is common for clinicians who are at odds with their patients to ignore those things that will help the comfort level of patients undergoing procedures. In this way they urge conformity to actual medical protocol while at the same exercising their power over patients Physicians have the opportunity and freedom to abuse patients verbally and in writing (medical records). Differing opinions about what patient care should entail between physician and patient may cause a physician to demean the feelings of patients. Patients have little recourse to combat this form of abuse. There is no vehicle by which the insults and emotional antagonism perpetrated on patients can be addressed in the clinical setting. Physicians have the patient chart with which they can defend their behavior while at the same time maligning and construing the patient response to unfair treatment. Suppression of patient opinion when that it is at odds with staff is paramount for healthcare workers. Physicians and nurses will begin to build the case for themselves when they first sense any dissatisfaction on the part of patients.

Character assassination of patients is what must be expected by anyone who dares to voice a demand for adequate and fair care when it is at odds with their patient's ideas.

"The drastic consequences of our mistakes, the repeated opportunities, the uncertainty about our own culpability when results are poor, and the medical and societal denial that mistakes must happen all result in an intolerable paradox for the physician. We see the horror of our own mistakes, yet we are given no permission to deal with the enormous emotional impact; instead we are forced to continue the routine of repeatedly making decisions, any one of which could lead us back into the same pit." New England Journal of Medicine Jan. 12, 1984

Even after the admission that mistakes must happen physicians refuse to accept the responsibility for them. They become unhappy because society doesn't give them permission to make mistakes. Even more pitiable is their lament that they are not taught how to deal with their mistakes in medical school! Making mistakes and coping with them is a life skill that everyone must have. Physicians must heal themselves of their fear of accountability.

In many instances medical therapy is violence. The motivation of medical violence may be different than those types of violent situations we normally think of. But make no mistake about it. Any procedure requiring anesthetic to make it tolerable is violence. The reasoning behind the act does not change the act itself. Should the outcome of therapy be positive what occasioned it was not. You can dress a wound any way you like but it remains a wound inflicted by one person to another. The gap between the violence of war or street violence narrows considerably when it derives from negligence and malpractice.

An act of malpractice has very long term consequences. It causes patients to become even more deeply involved with the mechanisms that have created his "misfortune". The more contact one has with the system the more opportunities for mistakes present themselves. The damage from one incident can mean a lifetime of insult and injury. Not infrequently the consequences of maltreatment may be greater than the original problem for which the patient sought help. Patients become bounced and battered from one area of specialization to another. Exiled from participating in the correction of a system they are none the less unable to leave it. It may be that battered woman syndrome has something in common with a battered patient syndrome. Our society is one which has made making the victim responsible for what befalls him an art form. This distortion of human thought is at its most refined when it passes between physician and patient. There is no public relations department powerful enough to undo the damage done to patients who are treated badly. The emotional abuse of patients is as much a part of healthcare facilities as the mortar and brick that hospitals are built with.

The new guidance system for care can be converted from provider produced stress to productive patient support. But the change can only be initiated by consumers. Before positive support for patients can become a reality, it must become provocative patient support. The change that our system has to undergo must be provoked by the vision of better more viable healthcare. Patients can and must give up passivity and replace it with active, enlivened ideas of what patient care must become.

Chapter 7

Medical Freedom

Doctors called upon to attend the sick cannot prescribe a cure unless they are first able to diagnosis the illness. Even before that, they must detect that the patient is ill. In the case of our freedoms, I can confidently say the patient is in grave danger.

Gerry Spence - From Freedom to Slavery

The current environment of healthcare is one where consumer choice is rapidly being eradicated. Restriction of choice means higher corporate profits. Some physicians support this by their own personal attitudes against patients who want to make their own choices. Consumers stand alone in advocating for freedom of choice. Reduction of choice has had a limiting negative monetary effect on physicians. But rather than speaking up to support consumers which would benefit both physician and patient, they attempt to compensate for it. The freedom to make money is a more important freedom than patient directed care for corporations. The culture of healthcare produces its own truths which are thrust on the American people as operative truths.

Physicians argue that patient directed care is not safe or effectual. This is untrue. Given an honest appraisal of options patients will choose what is right for them at the time. If this choice differs from the one a physician would choose for his patient, that doesn't make it wrong. Taking an active role in their care decreases fear and doubt in patients. It allows patients to feel more secure and right about the course of treatment. Most of the time patients will agree with the of choices that their physicians make. A few patients don't want to make treatment decisions preferring their doctor to make them. There is a wide range of patient involvement, and each individual must decide for himself what is best. Once that decision is made however, patients should not be criticized or pressured to change their mind. But this is a routine happening for patients who have made an unpopular choice.

In terms of insurance and HMOs consumers are in the unfavorable position of trying to regain lost freedom of choice. The time is long past when patients had true options about their care. It is no longer a matter of maintaining healthcare freedoms, but now a struggle to get them back. The connection between medical care and humanity no longer drives the system. Is it possible to reconnect with our humanity? Can consumers create enough momentum at the grass roots level to force change? Certainly this is at least as great a challenge as finding a cure for disease. Without the freedom of choice how is one to avail himself of the newest technology and therapies?

The dignity of freedom is inherent in human beings. Each patient can begin the journey back to freedom by expecting to be treated with dignity. When respect is lacking it is not only proper to insist on it but your right to do so. That is the first individual step. This may create shock on the part of clinicians, as it is something not often practiced in hospitals or offices. Healthcare workers are not used to such demands and believe it is their right to give or withhold respect for individual patients based on how they perceive patient behavior. Being confronted by someone who expects a fair and just level of interaction can also be unnerving to workers. As such, their response is usually defensive posturing. But if they are discomforted it is the result of their own poor behavior patterns. Consumers must stand together in their requirement for appropriate treatment from healthcare workers whether they be orderlies or chief of staff.

Dignity is an uncomplicated demand capable of being met by each and every person involved in the healthcare system today. It certainly doesn't require a high priced study commissioned by human resources departments. Dignity is understood by everyone, it does not demand training seminars. Clinicians and practitioners of every type can respond in a better way to consumers simply by making the choice to do so. Respect delayed is dignity purposely withheld.

Attitudes can only be changed by the people who hold the attitude. But workers who wish to change the way people are treated need to be supported in their efforts by their employers as well as patients. As for those who choose not to move healthcare forward it is best to leave them to their own way of doing things when possible. When one must be in the presence of these types, safety is the most important thing to pay attention to. Safety can be compromised by attitudes as surely as anything else.

Patients need to be involved in directing their care. Patients enduring chronic serious problems tend to be quite knowledgeable about their problems and may know about new treatment before their doctor does. They are also the first to spot inconsistencies in statement and treatment that are given to them by their doctors. Treatment must be consistent from beginning to end and always make sense in light of what has gone on before. Leaving patients out of the direction treatment takes can have far reaching consequences. Should not patients be allowed to direct treatment away from, and even encouraged to point out what can be harmful incongruities of care? No physician will openly admit that he intimidates patients thereby discouraging them from full involvement in their medical regime. But they do it all the time. That they deny it makes it no less real. There are enough things in the technical environs of modern clinics and hospitals that are intimidating in and of themselves. Doctors should be actively discouraging those aspects of care that they do have control over - themselves. Intimidation does not mean a win in the war on suffering. Consumers can and must nullify the use of intimidation whether by doctor, nurse or technician. Physicians take power because patients allow the transfer of power from themselves to their doctors. That "power drain" does not sustain the healing potential of patient or physician. The issue of who is in control is a struggle that must stop. Medical care consumers can refuse to be treated as ignorant and naive. The ineptitude of the system shows itself as providers project their feelings of inadequacy on their patients.

For the present consumers must set their course to overcoming the current system of inequities, greed, and its other inherent hazards. Patients must be on their guard as much as they are involved in the machinations of care. It is always possible that things will change for the better. But until that day arrives defensive consumerism is astute consumerism. It does not take a college degree to spot many of those things that are unsafe in today's healthcare climate. It is commonly said that patients should not be allowed to see their charts, and if they did they wouldn't understand it anyway. Physicians also insist that patients are easily frightened by "too much" information. Many people today have a scientific background or other technical skills that would enable them to understand most if not all of the chart material. It would certainly render them capable of learning what they did not know. Those without that type of educational background would be unencumbered with previous concepts that they would have to unlearn. But most importantly what patients don't know they can and should be taught. After all, what a patient is learning is about himself. Who has a greater right to know about you than you?

Today requires the patient to be steadfast in what they know to be right. If patients need help to maintain a strong defense they should call upon friends and family to help attain what is right and proper. To compromise what you believe to be right for yourself is to make a pact with everything that is wrong with the system today. Doctors walk away from your problems at the end of the day, you don't. Physicians believe if they see patients with the same problems day in and day out they have a very good idea of how their lives are affected. Actually they don't. They have a very good idea about how patients with like problems behave in a brief, contrived office visit. What must come from physicians is believability and credibility. For decades patients have felt as though they must prove illness to physicians in order to be believed. The burden of proof should be on physicians selling services not the patient. Degrees on the wall are no assurance of honesty, integrity and compassion. Yet those are the things most lacking in healthcare today. Physicians must be reduced in the eyes of the consumer to reflect the realities of the healthcare system. They must be seen as people, some good some bad but all struggling with a system that does not meet the needs of its participants.

Patients are seen as a class of people. A diverse class to be sure but they are one group. As a class of people they are subject to all of the prejudice applied to other groups. They are pre-judged, maligned, misunderstood and dismissed. No matter that consumers are in the majority, the oppressed often are. It is equality that patients must fight for. Other obstacles to care will fall like dominoes if ever equality between provider and patient is born, like the butterfly from its cocoon. This inequality will be the last to disappear because it is the most distasteful and buried the deepest in the psyche of an unfair system. Certainly injustice derived from feelings of superiority pushes long-suffering the farthest. As people who are prejudiced usually do, they hold themselves apart from those who are the subjects of their judgments. After decades of being removed from the tribulations of disease and the consequences of treatment what was once a small divide is now a canyon.

Humor and hope. One cannot exist without the other. But physicians are good at quashing both. Doctors and their staffs have been amusing themselves at the expense of their patients for years. But many patients find that physicians do foolish and sometimes funny things regularly. There are so many absurdities inherent in our system that one is always exposed to a cause for laughter. Patients who live with the severest challenges of disease often live the closest to laughter and can see it more quickly than others. The more one must confront that which exposes the true basis of life the more perspective one has. Humor evolves naturally from a correct perspective. This is a different humor than one finds in hospitals where doctors and nurses use humor to disguise how they feel about what they are doing. This is a genuine humor that shows an elevated way of being and knowing.

It is never necessary to accept the verdict of "no hope" when it comes from someone other than yourself. Patients and families let go when it is time to do so. No one else can tell them what is the right time. Physicians have patients who they feel are "better prospects" that they should be attending as opposed to those they consider a "waste of time". (His better prospects would undoubtedly pay his salary for a longer time.) No matter how shoddy the treatment, no matter how discouraging the present condition it is important that families be given their opportunity to hope until they choose not to. Choices about death are easier for physicians to make because they rely only on materiality to guide them. Anyone who has spent any length of time working in hospitals has seen patients recover when they have been given up on. Whether or not one sees these recoveries as miracles or the natural order of things they do happen. Patients and families that rely on prayer and spiritual support should never be denied the right as well as the time to use it. No one can know for sure what will happen. It is not a right of healthcare to destroy hope. Sometimes what is hoped for is the understanding of the real meaning of loss. Making families and patients give up on life prematurely, as patients see it, circumvents this right to the detriment of all involved. Taking away hope is not the kindness physicians have convinced themselves it is. To deprive people of their own individual process of understanding is always a cruelty.

It is standard thought by physicians that the observations that patients make about medical situations are incomplete at best. Just as patients are categorized in negative terms so are their perceptions and judgments about care. Such are the terms spontaneous remission and anecdotal evidence. Both phrases are useful to physicians. This is because they serve to stop patients from examining those things that physicians themselves do not understand. These terms are pejoratives as physicians commonly use them. Spontaneous remission does not explain anything. It is something to be said when physicians don't know what has happened. To counter their embarrassment when patients have untoward effects from treatment they use the dismissive phrase anecdotal evidence. As though all patient experiences are non-existent if they are not the product of a calculated scientific study. This is another manifestation of thought which says only labels applied by physicians are valid. Dead patients are sometimes referred to as anecdotal evidence when they are few in number. To say that the death of a patient is statistically insignificant is the extreme expression of ego. The same can be said for patients who survive when physicians say they won't. These are small minded excuses that patients realize are untrue.

The philosophical foundation of the healthcare system becomes solid reality in the lives of patients. Social mores rather than patient need dictate the direction and movement of the system. No where is this more apparent than in the area of pain management. There is no part of care that is more misapprehended than the unnecessary suffering of millions of people. In spite the of capabilities of healthcare and its potential physicians continue to perpetuate the dark ages of agony. More than 30 million people are experiencing chronic pain. Lost work days cost tens of billions of dollars every year. Chronic pain untreated is an economic disaster. The lack of commitment by physicians to treat suffering which they have the ability to effectively alleviate is shameful. And the mismanagement of pain control in children is unutterable in its sorrow.

The myths about pain that doctors continue to live by are:

- Chronic pain is to be endured, only acute short term pain is to be treated.

- Effective pain relief creates addicts.

- People who complain continually about being in pain are malingering. Especially those who are on disability or who file workman's compensation claims.

- They will lose licensure if pain medication is prescribed -even when appropriate- for long periods of time, losing their license to practice.

- Patients will demand more and more drugs as time passes to obtain relief.

The basis for the persistent adherence to these mistaken notions is as it normally is, physician ignorance, arrogance and lack of mercy for patients. Medical schools do not train physicians thoroughly enough about treating pain. The majority of physicians know very little about controlling it. Pain management is a clear, distinct field of focus. Rather than take the time to learn about pain and pain control, some physicians simply shrug their shoulders and ignore the subject. Very few patients in severe pain are able to find a physician with the skills that would afford them relief from lives of misery. Some patients especially those with limited funds give up the search in favor of suicide. To say some patients are driven to kill themselves because doctors choose not to do use available knowledge is not an exaggeration. Nor should patients have to wait until they are terminally ill to be considered "eligible" for pain relief.

The incidence of patients becoming addicted to those drugs they need for relief is very low. Taking drugs to influence a very specific physiological event is a far cry from the compulsion of drug taking to achieve a high. People using even strong analgesics on a long term basis do not experience a high. The addiction industry has done a great disservice to people who require narcotics to relieve unremitting pain. There are addicts who need treatment to be sure. But in their zeal to profitably treat the people who need it they may also label people with chronic pain addicts who are in fact not addicts. There are a few physicians who have tried to teach others about ways to manage pain. But their number is small and they receive little to no support from their colleagues. So most remain uneducated and are morally inadequate to deal with this issue. Physicians must take the initiative to learn what they do not know, it is their responsibility to do so. The information about how to control pain effectively is available. The compassionate clinician will find it and use it, those lacking compassion will find excuses to avoid taking the time to understand it.

The vast majority of patients with continuous pain can get good relief and in so doing resume active lives. Not giving the necessary medicines also means withholding patient productivity from society. Providing patients with what they need creates fear in physicians and they give into this fear at the expense of patients. Some prescriptions are monitored periodically by drug regulators to watch for abuses in the system. Doctors choose not to call attention to themselves by under prescribing and hurt patients trying to practice anonymously. This is not an issue that causes them concern. It is a cut and dried choice for them, physician comfort first and patient discomfort last. The facts do not support this kind of diffuse paranoia. A very few doctors do lose their license for the inappropriate medical management of pain. Physicians don't want to understand the real issues involved and the regulators support that viewpoint. The physician need for a deeper internal anonymity is externally exposed by the deepening pain of their patents. Expense of medication is also used as a reason to withhold drugs necessary for pain treatment as well. They will sometimes avoid prescribing costly drugs because to do so may bring unwanted attention to a physician. This happens even though the patient has an insurance company which is willing for their client to have a drug, because the more costly difficult alternative without medication would be hospitalization. Behavior of this type is a burden first on patients but also the system as a whole. This is the epitome of physician selfishness. Even more shameful is the withholding of proper pain management when the doctor himself has caused the suffering by his own ineptitude. Physicians should be thankful that even intense pain may actually be treatable but rarely is that an issue for them.

Physicians have a great deal of resources and power at their disposal. They do not hesitate to come together to influence those issues they really care about. If the majority of physicians believed treating chronic pain was beneficial to themselves in some way, it would be treated. Regulators can be educated as well as doctors. Legislators can change laws when convinced of the merit in doing so. Treating pain is not an issue of sympathy. It is based on scientific fact both for actual treatment and the reasons behind proper management. As long as physicians continue to ignore current and future data about pain management therapy millions will suffer needlessly. Many will go from productive citizen to a burden to society. Some will die for want of safe, effective treatment. As always the very young and elderly are the most easily ignored. Doctors and nurses avoid medicating the elderly because so often they hesitate to complain. It is common practice not to medicate for pain unless the patient is very vocal. But the elderly often don't complain because they don't want to be see as a bother to staff. Some hospitalized patients may be too weak or afraid to put on the call bell to summon the nurse. Other patients may become disoriented from illness or overwhelming fatigue from protracted pain and so can't convey what they need. But that doesn't mean they do not require pain medication. It is the responsibility of doctors and nurses to ensure that patients are resting comfortably.

Just as importantly, the relief of pain allows patients to use their energy and mind to spur healing. The extreme diminishing of a patient's physical resources reduce his prospects for healing. Living through pain is an enormous waste of healing potential. That effort should be directed toward improving one's condition not enduring it. Decreasing pain clarifies and frees energy to overcome and change difficult illness. While this idea is a source of ridicule for physicians and therapists common experience tells us people become more productive when suffering less not more.

The creation of a new paradigm rests on the efforts of individuals. The work of bringing forward new and better ways of thinking within the context of healthcare is the process of discovery. Discovery requires a problem to be solved and the impetus to solve it. The motivation for problem solving must be so important that it becomes an all absorbing issue. People suffering from a serious and protracted illness are driven to discover better ways of doing things to ensure survival and quality of life. As the days pass one by one, patients take those small steps that move them into a new way of perceiving their situation. They understand the need for a new paradigm when clinicians do not. People realize that they are laboring under the guise of a false ideal about what it means to be part of the healthcare system. But as consumers realize and accept their right and real place in the system the system itself will change. The change for patients is the recognition of a new role. For the system, change requires an acceptance of that role.

Discovery and subsequent change is not the exclusive arena of the "experts". The designations of discoverer and genius are labels put on people after a discovery is made. Many discoveries perhaps most, uncover principles that were already present. Discerning those new ways of regarding principles requires a dedicated devotion to the improvement of the status quo. Patients become absorbed in the creation of a better way of living by virtue of their continuing illnesses. Patients have all the raw materials they need to create an improved version of the healthcare environment. They are dedicated to not only themselves but family and friends who are an integral part of their lives. Patients are pioneers and discoverers to be acknowledged and valued as teachers and companions moving into the new millennium. If we match the courage of patients to the potential of the system, a new and better healthcare culture will evolve for the benefit of all.

The new guidance system for care can be converted from provider produced stress to productive patient support. But the change can only be initiated by consumers. Before positive support for patients can become a reality, it must become provocative patient support. The change that our system has to undergo must be provoked by consumers. In the eyes of providers patients are at their "best" when at their most passive. Patients can give up passivity and replace it with active, enlivened ideas of what patient care must become.

The average healthcare consumer understands the new direction our system must take because it is based on the oldest precepts of humankind. Healthcare is an issue of freedom. People need freedom to thrive and reach their potential, without it human beings can contribute nothing to themselves or society. Until the balance of power in the system is restored and patients regain the status of equality with the people charged with providing care, consumers must consider themselves less than equal to its practitioners. To quote one review of this manuscript by a senior editor "Ms. Lewis is a good writer who makes a strong argument for her cause. However, because we are connected with a large health care system, it is politically unfeasible for us to publish this book." Does the control of consumers by healthcare extend to the intimidation of publishers, thus restricting our freedom of speech? How is it that one woman who writes of her experiences with medical care can be threatening? Is our healthcare system so fragile that one person's opinion can undermine it? Patient care is also the outward manifestation of the system's goals. When the aim of the system is dignity, quality and equality, patients will be free to obtain true healthcare.

Until Americans come together under the same banner the dark days of healthcare will continue dim. Freedom for Consumers and Quit Managed Care should be the posture the people. More than any other aspect of a person freedom to know about themselves is a permanent right. But in this country consumers are denied the most intimate knowledge about themselves. Poorly constructed laws and backward public policy that make the attaining of medical records arduous if not impossible disgraces everyone who participates in this loss of consumer freedom. If a patient pays (or insurance on his behalf) for hospital care they should have access to all records generated with their identification number on it. All lab work, x-rays, incident reports, nursing notes, doctor's notes and consultations, physical therapies, medication administration, absolutely any and everything the patient wants to see. The same for office visits, all clinic and emergency care facilities. The most common way providers have of denying patients information is to tell they must obtain it from their doctor. In the first place doctors don't have all that information at their disposal and most will not make the effort to get it. This is how providers wear away the will of consumers to pursue what really belongs to them. Consumers pays very high prices for treatment and they deserve to know what they actually received and what they paid for. If something was done you should have a hard copy of what was done in its entirety.

We know of course that this simple, pure form of freedom would cause massive waves of apoplexy in the medical kingdom. Consumers aren't educated enough to understand the material and it would cost too much as clinicians believe. But the real question to be asked and answered is what are providers afraid of? They are afraid the public will understand what they are seeing. They fear that consumers will begin to truly understand what has been happening to them. That would be intolerable to both the medical and insurance industries. Keeping the American public ignorant is their best defense for a harmful but very profitable system.

How long will consumers keep the medical elite happy at their own expense? How long will unnecessary misery continue? It will exist as long as providers remain happy with the current direction of healthcare and until consumers demand and get an open, free and complete accounting of what is happening to them.

Can we reconnect with the humanity of today's healthcare? No. There is so little of it left in the system that our only hope is to start over and recreate the role of human hope in the system. Here we are fortunate for the human spirit is indomitable. Hope is the reality and hopelessness is not. Hard work and suffering go hand in hand wherever injustice is to be rooted out. The paradox is that patient and provider are juxtaposed. Providers seek to avoid humanity in the system because it decreases monetary profit, but what do human beings profit by if not their own humanity?

The medical care system is now composed of powerful alliances created to make great sums of money. The warning is clear to future reformers. Avoid power and its yearnings. The etiology of our healthcare morass is the drive to power. Patient empowerment is little more than a contest of wills at this time. Fighting back is just that-fighting-the goal of improved medical delivery is more important than fighting and power struggles. The authority of being human is far superior to anything power can conjure up. The honor of a just cause deserves more than power. The intention of raising the level of care and full access to information about it is a right created when human beings were created. Getting healthcare freedom is more than an issue. That some people resist the moral, legal and ethical commands of this right is the issue. Dishonor is attached to the strong, persistent attempts to deny citizens what they must have. It is time to return the deed of the human body back to the owner of that body. The blueprint for that body and all modifications performed on it must be returned, not secreted away in the bowels of clinics, hospitals and government institutions. People are better and higher than power. To create a new and better system method and motivation are paramount. In the words of one the world's greatest reformers Reverend Martin Luther King "Christ gave me the message, Gandhi gave me the method." Whatever one's inner orientation it is clear that what makes a human being great will make a system great. Until freedom is won there will be loss and pain. Some will survive to see some goals met and others will grow old and die before the reality of truth and fairness in healthcare appears. But the objective will never change and the cause remains fueled by the very ones who would cause its delay.

...Love supports the struggling heart until it ceases to
sigh over the world and begins to unfold its wings for heaven.
Mary Baker Eddy - c. 1875

About the Author

Cheryl Lewis—healthcare survivor, healthcare professional. Three decades of experience with patients is a secure foundation for Bedside Manners. As a victim of multiple surgeries followed by devastating infections and chronic rheumatic disease she conveys a carefully balanced viewpoint. Working, raising a family and coping with a rapidly changing healthcare culture created a wealth and depth of knowledge she has chosen to share with her readers. Practical experience however, is not enough. A deeply spiritual person she understands the value of solid psychological grounding and spiritual practice. Clarity, depth, and an ability to craft a narrative everyone will relate to. She is a remarkably talented and perceptive writer capable of following and chronicling American healthcare.

Printed in the United Kingdom
by Lightning Source UK Ltd.
112046UKS00001B/40